THE BRUNEVAL RAID

Operation *Biting* 1942

KEN FORD

First published in Great Britain in 2010 by Osprey Publishing,
Midland House, West Way, Botley, Oxford, OX2 0PH, UK
44–02 23rd St, Suite 219, Long Island City, NY 11101, USA
E-mail: info@ospreypublishing.com

Print ISBN: 978 1 84603 849 5
PDF e-book ISBN: 978 1 84908 297 6

Page layout by: Bounford.com, Cambridge, UK
Index by Sandra Shotter
Typeset in Sabon
Maps by Bounford.com, Cambridge, UK
Originated by PPS Grasmere Ltd
Printed in China through Worldprint

10 11 12 13 14   10 9 8 7 6 5 4 3 2 1

A CIP catalogue record for this book is available from the British Library.

THE WOODLAND TRUST

Osprey Publishing are supporting the Woodland Trust, the UK's leading
woodland conservation charity, by funding the dedication of trees.

IMPERIAL WAR MUSEUM COLLECTIONS

Many of the photos in this book come from the Imperial War Museum's
huge collections which cover all aspects of conflict involving Britain and
the Commonwealth since the start of the twentieth century. These rich
resources are available online to search, browse and buy at
www.iwmcollections.org.uk. In addition to Collections Online, you can
visit the Visitor Rooms where you can explore over 8 million photographs,
thousands of hours of moving images, the largest sound archive of its
kind in the world, thousands of diaries and letters written by people in
wartime, and a huge reference library. To make an appointment, call
(020) 7416 5320, or e-mail mail@iwm.org.uk.

Imperial War Museum www.iwm.org.uk

EDITOR'S NOTE

For ease of comparison between types, Imperial/American
measurements are used almost exclusively throughout this book.
The following data will help in converting the Imperial/American
measurements to metric:

1 mile = 1.6km

1lb = 0.45kg

1yd = 0.9m

1ft = 0.3m

1in = 2.54cm/25.4mm

1gal = 4.5 liters

1 ton (US) = 0.9 tonnes

FOR A CATALOGUE OF ALL BOOKS PUBLISHED BY OSPREY MILITARY
AND AVIATION PLEASE CONTACT:

Osprey Direct, c/o Random House Distribution Center,
400 Hahn Road, Westminster, MD 21157
Email: uscustomerservice@ospreypublishing.com

Osprey Direct, The Book Service Ltd, Distribution Centre,
Colchester Road, Frating Green, Colchester, Essex, CO7 7DW
E-mail: customerservice@ospreypublishing.com

www.ospreypublishing.com

CONTENTS

INTRODUCTION

Prior to World War II, both Britain and Germany had independently discovered that radio waves could be used to detect aircraft. Thus began the race to develop and deploy radar before the other side could put the process to effective use. For the first year or so of the conflict, each side thought that it was leading the race.

Britain was confident that it was well ahead in the radar war and in a sense it was. Although German radar was of a high quality and as advanced as British equipment, its application and administration was not as effective. The Nazi military still regarded their role as being offensive rather than defensive and tried to employ the new technology to that end. Britain, in contrast, was more inclined to use the new equipment to protect itself from the horrors of aerial bombardment and had effectively integrated radar into its inter-service defence network. It had set up systems to exploit the information gained from radar. In this respect it was well ahead of Germany.

Britain had begun its research into what was eventually to become known as radar in 1935. At the time its scientists were studying the possibility of destroying enemy aircraft by means of 'death rays'. Such an idea might seem fanciful now, but in the 1930s the advances made in science appeared to show that anything was possible. A common fear was that enemy bombers could suddenly appear overhead to wreak havoc on civilian populations and every method that could lead to their detection and destruction was given serious thought.

A leading member of the committee at that time looking into air defence was a scientist from the Radio Research Station, Robert Watson-Watt. He concluded that whilst it was impossible to destroy enemy aircraft through radio waves, it should be possible to detect them by bouncing radio energy back from the aircraft's metal body. He was led to this conclusion by investigations made by one of his colleagues, Arnold Wilkins, who was intrigued by observations made by Post Office radio engineers that aircraft flying though a high-frequency radio beam caused the beam to become distorted. An experiment was set up to prove this point to RAF observers in

February 1935 and the results were so impressive that funds were made available to develop the idea. The process was termed Radio Detection Finding (RDF) and the whole procedure was considered so revolutionary and important that it was given a Top Secret level of security.

The early development of RDF, which eventually became known as RAdio Detection And Ranging – RADAR (later to lose its capital letters and become 'radar'), was carried out by Watson-Watt's team at the Telecommunications Research Establishment (TRE) at Bawdsey Manor in Suffolk. Within a year a working system had been developed. It used transmitters radiating a pulsed sequence of radio waves in the 20MHz–30MHz band, which were reflected by aircraft flying into the beam. The reflections would then be detected on receivers located adjacent to the transmitters. The system demonstrated itself capable of detecting aircraft up to a distance of 130km. This proven arrangement was then integrated into Britain's air defences and, by the time that war was declared, a string of these radar stations, known as Chain Home, were located along the east and south coast of England and the east coast of Scotland.

The Chain Home stations did valuable work identifying German attacks during the Battle of Britain in 1940. The system would pick up incoming enemy aircraft whilst they were well out to sea and its controllers would vector RAF fighters to intercept them. The arrangement worked well but its

The buildings of Le Presbytère at Bruneval. The farm complex was used as a barracks for the Luftwaffe signallers and operators manning the radar sites. After the raid the area was fortified with the addition of Tobruk machine-gun posts and concrete gun emplacements. (Ken Ford)

Home are the conquering heroes. A group of delighted paratroopers from C Company arrive alongside the *Prinz Albert* in the Solent after their return from the raid on Bruneval. This successful airborne operation against Hitler's occupied Europe became the first battle honour awarded to the Parachute Regiment. (IWM H17358)

effectiveness and importance was not immediately realized by the Luftwaffe, which allowed the RAF to have the upper hand during a most crucial period.

Further development work in Britain saw improvements in radar ground control interception of enemy aircraft using rotating antennae and higher frequencies. Other smaller airborne systems were engineered to allow aircraft-to-aircraft interception and the detection of submarines by aircraft whilst the boats were on the surface. Perhaps the most important development in the history of radar was the invention of the cavity magnetron by John Randall and Harry Boot at Birmingham University in 1940. This small device allowed for the generation of microwave frequencies much more efficiently, and enabled Britain to develop radar in the 3GHz band. These ultra-high frequencies enabled the detection of smaller objects using much more compact antennae and consequentially freed up the deployment of radar apparatus from the cumbersome equipment of the previous years. The cavity magnetron was the single most important invention in the history of radar. This remarkable piece of apparatus was given as a free gift to the USA, along with several other inventions, as part of an inducement to enter the war on the side of the British.

In the meantime, Britain was slow to appreciate that Germany and many other countries were also making progress in the field of radio waves. Each had scientists working on equipment that operated at shorter and shorter wavelengths, and each was very protective of the knowledge gained by its researchers. There was little interchange between countries on developments, all therefore progressed in something of a vacuum, so Britain entered the war with many of its important scientific advisers believing that the country was far ahead of any of its rivals and certainly well ahead of Germany.

Radar was not the only field in which other nations were making remarkable progress and often led the way. Germany was at the forefront in tank, aircraft and weapons design and was innovative in the way these new machines were being deployed. Air power was fundamental to the success of Germany's 'Blitzkrieg' tactics and its experimentation in the use of airborne troops gave the country a powerful edge over other belligerent nations. Nor was the use of paratroops confined to the Nazi regime, for Soviet Russia had for years been experimenting with airborne forces. On a trip to Russia in 1936, General Wavell had watched a demonstration of Stalin's air power. He witnessed a whole battalion of 1,200 men, led by a general and complete with 150 machine-guns and eighteen light field guns, successfully drop on its target. 'If I had not witnessed the descents,' he later wrote, 'I could not have believed such an operation possible.' Britain lagged well behind these new developments and at the start of the war had no airborne forces of its own.

ORIGINS

Before World War II, Germany had made great advances in the field of radio. By the outbreak of the conflict it had perfected a system of guiding its bombers to their targets at night using narrow beams. Called 'Knickebein', it allowed bombers to fly along a precise radio beam pointed at its target. If the aircraft deviated from the prescribed bearing, the signal would change and the pilot was able to correct his direction in order to stay on the beam. Once over the target the bomber intercepted another beam, which became the signal for the warplane to drop its bombs. The system was used operationally against Britain in 1940 and was gradually perfected to become first 'X-Gerät', using three intercept beams for more accuracy and then 'Y-Gerät', which utilized a single-beam method that triggered a response from the aircraft so the ground controller could determine its position and initiate the point at which bombs should be dropped. All three methods were very accurate navigational tools, far in advance of anything Britain had to offer.

Precise though these systems were – their pinpoint accuracy was amply demonstrated in the destruction of Coventry on the night of 14/15 November 1940 – they were susceptible to jamming by British countermeasures as its scientists gradually discovered more about how they worked. By the end of 1940 most enemy efforts to use the beams had been jammed. Germany was then obliged to turn its 'blitz' on Britain against major sites that were easily recognizable from the air, such as London and the large ports of Southampton, Portsmouth, Bristol and Plymouth. It was thus forced to carry out area, rather than precision, bombing.

Leading the task of discovering what Germany was doing in the field of radio was a civilian scientist attached to the Air Ministry's Scientific Information Branch, Dr Reginald Victor Jones. It was fortunate that the nation had such a man as Jones working in this sphere at that time, for he had a remarkable ability to predict what logical developments could be achieved by the enemy, even before they had become a reality. It was this deductive technical capacity of Dr Jones's that allowed Britain to keep track of the Germans in the evolution of radar. Germany's use of narrow radio beams to aid navigation prompted Jones into thinking that they were also using narrow beams for radar, even though many at the top of the scientific world in Britain felt otherwise.

In fact Germany was, as Jones predicted, making startling progress with the idea of using radio beams in the area of radio detection systems. However, unlike the British the scientists and engineers working in this field all belonged to commercial companies and each developed their work more or less in isolation. Systems were built and then demonstrated to the military, rather than progressing in concert with the requirements of the German

Kriegsmarine and the Luftwaffe. This tended to slow down advances and lead to inter-service rivalries.

By the time war broke out the Kriegsmarine was sponsoring radar work and had on its major warships a serviceable short-wave system (60cm) built and developed by the electronics company GEMA. Known as 'Seetakt', it was capable of locating surface ships, in perfect conditions, up to 160km away, but was primarily designed for ranging purposes rather than for detection. Over 200 Seetakt radars were built, a number of which were used for coastal defence. Another system developed by GEMA for the German Navy used long-wave technology and worked in the 2.5-metre waveband at 120MHz. This became known as the 'Freya' early warning radar system. It had a range of almost 160km but, unlike the British Chain Home system, could not determine the altitude of any intruding aircraft. The Luftwaffe had little knowledge of these developments until 1938 for the German Navy kept the development work secret. Once Generalfeldmarschall Göring got to hear of Freya's ability to detect aircraft, the Luftwaffe immediately ordered a number of Freya systems for its own use.

By mid-1940 Britain knew that Germany had some practical radar, but had few details of its size and performance. Intelligence suggested that a system called Freya was employed in France although what it looked like and how it was used was still not known. Dr Jones needed the answers to these questions and knowledge of the actual frequencies Freya operated over, but first a working system had to be located so that it could be carefully studied. There was some suspicion that some kind of radar station on the Cherbourg Peninsula in France had detected the destroyer HMS *Delight* when it was 30km off Portland Bill and then directed German bombers to intercept and sink the warship. Aerial photo-reconnaissance later indicated that there was an unknown installation close by a compound near to Cherbourg that included known X-Gerät and Y-Gerät transmitters, which might be Freya radar.

Further aerial pictures gave Jones the evidence he was looking for. Careful study of two sequential photographs made on 22 February 1941 showed a rotating antenna around 9m high. In the meantime an assistant of Dr Jones's, Derrick Garrard, had taken a suitable radio receiver down to the south coast and was listening for enemy radar transmissions. Two days later he succeeded in hearing Freya transmissions around the 120MHz frequency. The two pieces of evidence proved to the Air Ministry that the Germans had radar and were using it.

During the next few months more and more intelligence, supported by technical deductions made by Jones, all indicated that Freya was being used as a long-distance directional radar. It also indicated the existence of another type of radar, called 'Würzburg', which was being employed in conjunction with Freya to give short-range information on the height and bearing of intruding aircraft. Intelligence suggested numbers of these two radars working together made up an effective defence line across northern Europe. The Kammhuber Line, as it was called, controlled intercepting German night-fighter groups and directed them on to incoming British bombers. The system was most effective and proving to be costly to RAF Bomber Command.

Jones quickly realized that the technical make-up of Würzburg would need to be analysed so that some sort of jamming arrangements could be employed to counter its effects. It was clear that Würzburg was one of the most important of the enemy's radars, employing the latest German developments. There was much evidence of its existence, for intelligence sources had claimed to have seen a mysterious parabolic antenna in Germany

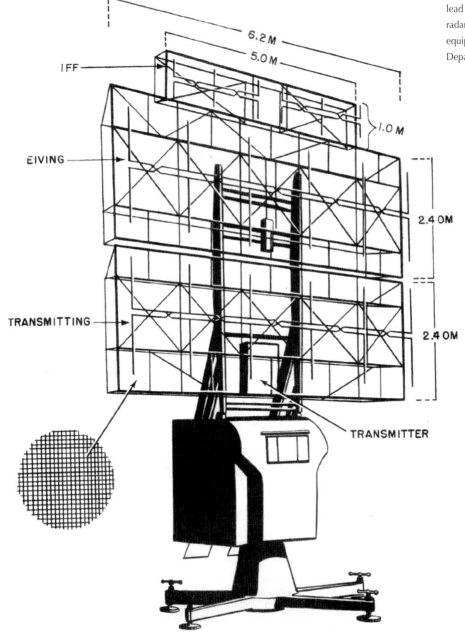

Diagram of a German Freya radar of the type based at Bruneval. It was the discovery of this type of installation at Bruneval that helped the British locate the presence of a Würzburg radar on the same site. Experts had reasoned that the inherent efficiency of the Germans would most likely lead them to put the newer radar close by existing Freya equipment. (US War Department)

M

LAERMENTS

SMALL BLACK OBJECT

The picture that initiated the planning of Operation *Biting*. This photograph, from the archives of Combined Operations, highlights the 'small black object' that aroused so much interest in the Photographic Interpretation Section when it was looking for the location of a Würzburg radar installation. It was nothing more than a speck on a photographic plate, but it was the first indication that the radar existed. (Crown Copyright)

and listening groups from the TRE had detected pulsed German transmissions opposite Dover in the 50cm waveband at around 570MHz. The information pointed to the possibility that the enemy was employing Würzburg to detect incoming British aircraft as they approached the French coast. Further investigation by scientists from TRE in aircraft fitted with high-powered radio receivers had detected transmissions in the 50cm waveband all along the Channel coast.

Jones now lobbied for aerial reconnaissance photographs to be studied in detail to find one of these elusive and mysterious parabolic antennae. It was accepted that the apparatus worked in the 50cm band and transmitted a pulsed beam with a repetition rate of between 3,600 and 4,000 per second. From this it was relatively straightforward to deduce that the radar had a range of about 40km. Therefore to cover the whole coastline there would have to be one station every 80km along the French coast. The likely sites were narrowed down by employing the theory that the Germans would apply themselves to their normal dictate of convenience and security and locate their Würzburgs in the same compounds as their Freyas.

On 15 November 1941, sortie T/953 by the RAF Photo-Reconnaissance Unit took pictures of the coastline north of Le Havre in France. The Central Interpretation Unit (CIU) staff at Medmenham found Photograph 02Y to be of great interest, for it showed a Freya station located on top of the cliffs along the coast near Cap d'Antifer. Study of the photograph showed a fairly standard layout for the site with the usual large antenna emplacements. Dr Jones's insistence that these sites should be carefully examined prompted his assistant, Dr F. C. Frank, to scrutinize the photograph in greater detail.

Dr Frank pointed out that a path led along the cliff edge for some distance towards a large villa. It stopped, however, a few metres short of the house in a large loop. At the end of the loop was a small black object, no more that a tiny pinprick on the 12.5cm by 12.5cm contact print that the doctor was studying. Frank suggested that someone had considered it necessary to make a track from the main Freya station to this object. Might it therefore, he reasoned, itself be a radar of some sort?

When the discovery was reported to Jones he used his influence to get the object photographed in more detail. He contacted the CIU and asked for low-level pictures of the installation at Cap d'Antifer, explaining that what he was looking for might resemble a large electric bowl fire. On 4 December 1941 Flight Lieutenant Tony Hill DFC made a photographic reconnaissance sortie over the site and saw the apparatus in question, reporting that it did indeed look like an electric bowl fire. Unfortunately the photographs he took missed the object itself and were inconclusive. Undaunted, he successfully repeated the flight the next day at great personal risk and brought back two incredibly detailed pictures of the installation.

Jones was overjoyed when he received the photographs for they confirmed the existence of Würzburg in the form that he had expected. Its antenna was a parabolic dish with a diameter of around 3m. Its equipment appeared to be housed in a small shed located at the base of the aerial. The whole installation was situated remote from any other building in a low-banked hollow. Close by was a nineteenth-century villa, which no doubt housed the technicians manning the radar installation. The site itself was no more than 100 metres from the cliff edge, with a clear view out to sea.

As Jones and Frank studied the terrain surrounding the radars, they were struck by the openness of the compound. It was perched close to the cliff's edge with a path running down to a small beach. To its rear was wide-open countryside with no town of any significant size nearby. Its vulnerability to attack was plain to see. The idea began to form in their minds of a raid being mounted to steal the radar. The component parts of the Würzburg if studied at first hand would yield any number of enemy secrets. Jones was at first loath to suggest anything that might cause any loss of life, but possession of the radar could help stifle the enemy's advances in the use of radar and might help shorten the war. It was a risk that, on balance, was worth taking.

NOVEMBER 15 1941

Freya station discovered at Bruneval

DECEMBER 4–5 1941

Radar identified at Bruneval

INITIAL STRATEGY

After the British retreat from the mainland of Europe via Dunkirk in June 1940, Britain was besieged by Nazi forces just 42km away in France and the Low Countries. To harness the country's spirit of resistance, Prime Minister Winston Churchill urged the setting up of special forces with the specific task of striking back at the enemy across the Channel.

A full-scale invasion would be out of the question for some time, so special units, such as the commandos, were raised to raid and harass the enemy at times and places he would least expect. To co-ordinate these special tasks a new organization was set up in July 1940, which was intended to integrate small-scale land, sea and air operations against enemy-held territories. This new department, Combined Operations (CO), was originally headed by the architect of the 1918 Zeebrugge raid, Admiral of the Fleet Lord Roger Keyes, but by October 1941 the young and energetic Lord Louis Mountbatten, a cousin of the king, had taken over command. The organization had no fighting troops of its own, but consisted of background staff whose job was to plan operations and to develop ideas and equipment with which to harass the enemy in any way possible. Its HQ planning teams evaluated any suggestions, co-ordinated a workable plan and calculated the units required, before deciding whether or not to forward the proposal to the Combined Chiefs of Staff Committee for permission to execute the raid.

It was to COHQ that Dr Jones's request for a raid to be mounted against the German radar site at Bruneval near Cap d'Antifer was put in December 1941. It was met with a great deal of enthusiasm, for the raid was just the type of enterprise that Combined Operations were looking for. The attack was not intended merely to be an in-and-out punitive foray, for it had a worthwhile objective that would contribute to the nation's security. It was also an operation that would cause great disquiet within the Nazi hierarchy, a thought that would please the Prime Minister immensely. The location of the radar site on top of a cliff adjacent to the beach at Bruneval made it a most attractive location both for landings and embarkation; a commando unit could be set down and embarked with few problems. This was a raid that, if executed with some dash and a lot of determination, had a very good chance of complete success.

The obvious method of attack and withdrawal was by sea. With a landing beach close by it was clearly the simplest and most cost-effective way, but there was another method that might be used, which had an element of politics about it. Britain's fledgling airborne forces were looking for some way of redeeming themselves after their disastrous first operation in Italy and this raid might be the very thing they too were looking for.

Britain's first airborne unit began its life as No. 2 Commando in 1940, selected and trained specifically for parachute operations. On 21 November of that year it was redesignated 11th Special Air Service Battalion and by 17 December the battalion felt that it was ready for action, having completed all of its parachute training and demonstrated its ability in a number of exercises. It was felt that this new type of warfare needed to be tested under fire and a raid was planned to test its methods of deployment, its equipment and the aircraft it used. On 7 February 1941 a small group from 11th SAS Battalion was parachuted into Italy to attack the aqueduct across the River Tragino near Calitri in the province of Campania. It was intended that the raiders would demolish the aqueduct and then withdraw to the coast near the mouth of the River Sele to be evacuated by the submarine HMS *Triumph*.

Flight Lieutenant Tony Hill's famous oblique photograph of the Würzburg installation at Bruneval. From this one picture everything that was suspected about the radar was confirmed. Its existence and vulnerability on the cliffs above a small beach so excited Dr Jones that he pressed for a raid to be mounted to steal its secrets. (IWM D12870)

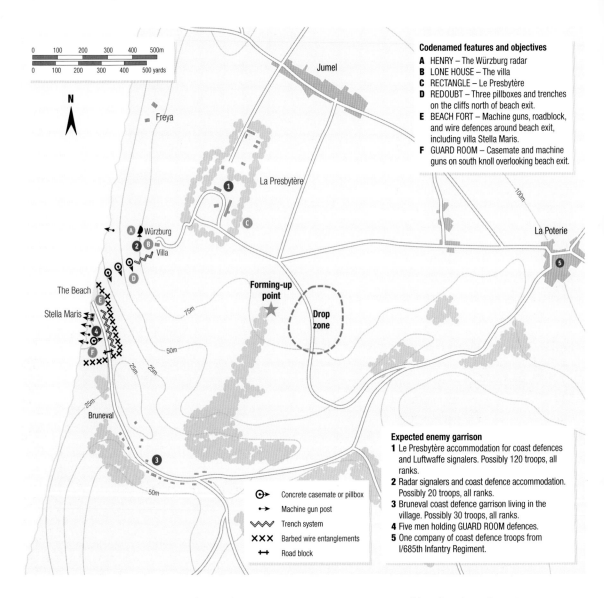

Codenamed features and objectives

A HENRY – The Würzburg radar
B LONE HOUSE – The villa
C RECTANGLE – Le Presbytère
D REDOUBT – Three pillboxes and trenches on the cliffs north of beach exit.
E BEACH FORT – Machine guns, roadblock, and wire defences around beach exit, including villa Stella Maris.
F GUARD ROOM – Casemate and machine guns on south knoll overlooking beach exit.

Concrete casemate or pillbox
Machine gun post
Trench system
Barbed wire entanglements
Road block

Expected enemy garrison

1 Le Presbytère accommodation for coast defences and Luftwaffe signalers. Possibly 120 troops, all ranks.
2 Radar signalers and coast defence accommodation. Possibly 20 troops, all ranks.
3 Bruneval coast defence garrison living in the village. Possibly 30 troops, all ranks.
4 Five men holding GUARD ROOM defences.
5 One company of coast defence troops from I/685th Infantry Regiment.

The raid was not a great success. Several loads of vital equipment were lost and some paratroopers were dropped wide of the mark and failed to reach the target. The aqueduct was, however, eventually destroyed along with an adjacent bridge, but everyone who took part in the raid, except one man, was captured and made a prisoner of war. Within a short time the aqueduct was repaired and the region's water supplies remained unaffected throughout. Nonetheless, although the raid was not the *coup de main* and national morale builder that had been hoped for, several important lessons were learned from the operation, the main one being that there was a future for airborne troops, and so further steps were taken to build up a parachute force.

On 5 September 1941 HQ 1st Parachute Brigade was formed, with Brigadier Richard Gale at its head. Its three battalions came into being the same month, with the 1st Battalion being created from the already trained

11th Special Air Service Battalion and the 2nd and 3rd Battalions raised from army volunteers. A month later, on 31 October 1941, the 1st Airborne Division became operational, with Major General Frederick 'Boy' Browning as its General Officer Commanding (GOC) and with the 1st Parachute Brigade placed under command. A month later still, the 1st Airlanding Brigade, formed from the 31st Infantry Brigade Group, joined the division. By the end of 1941 Britain had an airborne division in being, but not yet ready for offensive operations.

With these new airborne units being raised and gradually made ready for action at the start of 1942, there was a pressing need to have some success attached to parachute forces. Their profile required raising in the eyes of the public and experience needed to be gained from contact with the enemy. When Combined Operations planners considered the proposed raid on the radar station at Bruneval it was suggested that the raid might be undertaken not by commandos, but by paratroops. Their swift, silent approach from the sky would add an element of surprise to the operation and their

Major John Frost on board the Combined Operations support ship *Prinz Albert* after his return from Bruneval. He is recounting the raid to the GSO1 of the 1st Parachute Division. (IWM H17349)

embarkation by sea would ensure that the whole enterprise involved all three services to become a truly combined operation. Mountbatten agreed and so did the Chiefs of Staff Committee when the proposal was put to them. The only problem was, would the paras be trained and ready in time?

With permission granted for the operation to take place it became necessary for COHQ to plan the raid in detail. One factor that was very hard to determine was the strength of the enemy defences and the opposition that the raiders might have to face. Photo-reconnaissance could indicate only so much; the finer details would have to be filled in by agents in France. Fortunately there was a brilliant agent working from Paris, Gilbert Renault (code name 'Rémy'), whose network Confrérie Notre-Dame covered the whole of northern France. Rémy in turn had a very special recruit called Roger Dumont (code name 'Pol'), who conveniently had an agent working with him who was based at Le Havre, just 29km south of Bruneval and the radar station.

On 24 January 1942 Rémy received a coded radio message from his Special Operations Executive (SOE) controllers in London containing an urgent request for information about the enemy around Bruneval and the coast. They wanted to know a number of things, including the location of any machine-guns defending the cliff road; all the other defences present in the area; the number and state of preparedness of the German defenders; where enemy troops were quartered; and the positions of any barbed-wired areas. This was information that could be ascertained only by agents actually visiting the area. Rémy passed the request on to Pol, who in turn sought the help of his agent in Le Havre, Charles Chauveau, code name 'Charlemagne'.

Charles Chauveau was a garage proprietor with a permit to use his car in the region of Seine-Inférieure, the area around Le Havre. When Pol told him of the British need for details about the Germans at Bruneval, Charlemagne responded with enthusiasm. He already knew the owners of the hotel in the village quite well and reassured Pol that they were friendly to the Allied cause. He was sure that they would have much useful information to give them.

Charlemagne was right; the owners of the Hotel Beauminet located at the top end of the village, Monsieur and Madame Venniers, had a great deal of information to give to the two agents when they visited. They told them that the Luftwaffe personnel garrisoning the radar site were housed in the great rectangle of farm buildings called Le Presbytère, which was situated just north of the villa on the cliffs. In Bruneval itself there was a platoon of German troops led by a sergeant maintaining the guard on the route down to the beach. They were housed in the hotel and in a villa overlooking the beach. Two bunkers, each containing a machine-gun, guarded the beach exit. The road itself was barred by barbed-wire emplacements and the beach and the grass verge bordering the road were mined.

Chauveau and Dumont decided they would try to have a look at the beach for themselves, even though the Venniers warned them that it was forbidden. Their bravado paid off, for the bored German sentry guarding the road allowed them down to the sea, believing the story that Dumont was a student from Paris and wished to see the ocean before he returned to the city. The guard raised the barrier-post on the road and let them pass through to the tiny beach nestling beneath the cliffs. The 'Achtung Minen' notices proved to be just for show, for the German followed closely behind the two men and allowed them onto the shingle. The Frenchmen behaved courteously, engaging in some friendly chitchat to put the sentry at ease. On the way back the German walked casually over the other supposedly mined area near the road with little caution whilst the two agents noted the exact positions of the machine-guns defending the exit from the sea. The two Frenchmen had seen all that there was to see and retreated back to the hotel and then on to Le Havre. The reconnaissance mission had been a great success and the required information about the area was quickly beamed back to SOE in London and then to COHQ, who now had sufficient details to go ahead with planning the fine detail of the raid.

Once the decision had been made to use paratroopers for the operation, Major-General Browning and Brigadier Richard Gale were notified on 14 January that one company, with attendant sappers, would be required for training in combined operations with a view to carrying out a raid. The two

Captain Ross speaking to some of his group on the beach in Dorset during a training exercise. Ross was Major Frost's second in command during the raid, with the added task of holding the road leading down to the beach at Bruneval against an enemy attack from the village. (IWM 17414)

**JANUARY 20
1942**

**Major Frost's
company starts
special
training**

senior officers now had to decide which of their troops would take part. Their most experienced parachutists belonged to the 1st Parachute Battalion, which was formed from the 11th SAS, but Gale decided on a company from his 2nd Battalion. C Company had been in training for almost four months and its men had acquitted themselves well. The 2nd Battalion's commander, Lieutenant-Colonel E. W. C. Flavell, had earlier decided to form C Company from volunteers from many of the Scottish regiments. These Scotsmen arrived at the training camp seemingly in better shape than most of the others and they quickly began to forge themselves into an impressive group; 'an outstanding body of men' was how C Company's commander Major John Frost described them.

By the third week in January COHQ had evolved a working plan for the raid, now called Operation *Biting*, which had been put to the three services. On 20 January, Major Frost was briefed that his company was to embark on a special programme of training that would involve them moving south to Tilshead Camp on Salisbury Plain, the home of the recently formed Glider Pilot Regiment. To preserve secrecy, Frost was told nothing of the raid but that his unit would be training for a demonstration to the War Cabinet towards the end of February. Bad weather, most notably freezing temperatures and heavy snow, delayed this move from Yorkshire until 24 January.

The air component of the raid was in three parts. First, the RAF was required to transport the parachutists to their objective at Bruneval in France; second, it was required to distract the enemy's attention by diversionary

Part of the flotilla of motor gun boats that took part in the Bruneval Raid, berthed alongside the *Prinz Albert* in the Solent. (IWM H17361)

raids, and third, it needed to provide fighter cover during daylight hours to the naval forces employed in the operation. Group Captain Sir Nigel Norman was appointed to co-ordinate the training and preparation of the RAF units for the raid. Other RAF groups would provide fighter cover and bomber diversion. Group Captain Norman specialized in providing air support for the army and had, on 15 January 1942, raised 38 Wing RAF Army Co-operation Command to provide transport aircraft for airborne operations. The wing's first Order of Battle consisted of No. 296 and No. 297 Squadrons, both based at Netheravon in Wiltshire. However, neither of these squadrons were immediately available for operations when orders for the raid were given to Group Captain Norman just one week after he had raised the wing, so he was assigned 12 aircraft from No. 51 Squadron Bomber Command to use in the operation.

No. 51 Squadron was one of the many night bomber units that had been flying operations over Europe since 1940. Its commander, Wing Commander Percy Charles Pickard, was well known to the British public from his appearance in the propaganda film *Target for Tonight*, in which he was shown flying the Wellington bomber 'F' for Freddie on an operational sortie over Germany. Pickard was a very experienced bomber pilot who had already been awarded the Distinguished Flying Cross (DFC) and the Distinguished Service Order (DSO) and was later to earn a Bar to add to his DSO for his part in Operation *Biting*.

The Bruneval operation as a whole was under the supreme command of the Commander-in-Chief Portsmouth, Admiral Sir William 'Bubbles' James. Admiral James had acquired his unusual nickname from his having sat as the child model for the painting *Bubbles* created by his grandfather, the celebrated artist John Millais. The painting, now in the Lady Lever Art Gallery in Liverpool, was to gain worldwide acclaim through its use in an advertisement for Pears soap. Commander F. N. Cook of the Royal Australian Navy was designated Naval Force Commander reporting to Admiral James and it was his task to co-ordinate the naval craft that would evacuate the paratroopers from the beach at Bruneval and bring them back across the Channel to Portsmouth. Commander Cook at that time was in command of HMS *Tormentor*, a land-based Royal Navy Combined Operations School that was set up in August 1940 as a motor gun boat (MGB) operational and maintenance base. MGBs from this small unit located on the River Hamble close to Southampton were to be used to help embark the raiders and their landing craft from Bruneval.

The information gained by the French agents was useful but did not paint the whole picture of the enemy forces that might be encountered on the raid. Chauveau and Dumont had identified two bunkers containing machine-guns overlooking the beach at Bruneval, but there were others. Photo-reconnaissance sorties over the area showed there was a line of three emplacements linked by a network of trenches that guarded the path that led from the road near the beach up to the villa alongside the Würzburg site. Two further weapons pits were located along the cliff edge between the Würzburg and the Freya positions.

The model of the villa and Würzburg at Bruneval made especially for the raid. On this model the finer details of the attack on the house and radar installation were worked out by Frost and his junior officers. (Crown Copyright)

Careful study of the pictures and an appreciation of the information gained by the French agents indicated that some of the local defence of the site was down to Luftwaffe personnel on the ground. A company of coast defence infantry, garrisoned locally at La Poterie, looked after the coastline in the vicinity of the radar sites. At Bruneval some of these troops were located in the complex of farm buildings just to the north of the villa at Le Presbytère and would most likely be the first of the enemy to oppose the landings. The platoon of army troops garrisoned in the nearby village of Bruneval was there to guard against landings from the sea. Once roused by the arrival of low-flying aircraft and the sounds of gunfire at the radar site, they would no doubt move to man their positions guarding the beach and would provide stiff opposition to any withdrawal once the raid was completed.

PLANNING AND TRAINING

By the end of January the forces allocated to Operation *Biting* had been identified and the task of detailed planning and training was under way. For the Royal Navy it was a matter of helping to train Frost's paratroopers in embarkation techniques and arranging for the flotilla of vessels to be offshore at the appropriate time. For the men of C Company, 2nd Parachute Battalion, they had to become proficient in landing by parachute and regrouping on target, accomplishing the objectives of the raid and getting out again with as few casualties as possible. For the RAF, No. 51 Squadron had to convert its Whitley bombers to carry parachutists, train with them as airborne transport and get the men to their target safely and on time. Other RAF units would conduct diversionary raids and fighter cover as required.

Operation *Biting* was not a punitive raid; it had a much greater purpose than merely to terrorize a German garrison and take prisoners. Its main objective was to steal radar equipment and this in itself required expert personnel and engineering support. C Company was the brute force of the enterprise, intent on imposing its will on the German defenders and marshalling its men to ensure that the theft was successful. Expertise in engineering aspects was provided by a detachment from the Airborne Division's Air Troop Royal Engineers under the command of Lieutenant Dennis Vernon. Crucial to the operation was the inclusion of a radar expert who could determine what parts of the radar equipment were valuable to the objective and what were not. That expert was RAF Flight Sergeant Charles Cox.

Flt Sgt Cox was a technician at the Chain Home radar station at Hartland Point in north Devon with a good working knowledge of RDF. He was regarded as being one of the best radar mechanics in Britain. On 1 February 1942 Cox was called to the Air Ministry in London to see Air Commodore Tait. The senior officer asked him to volunteer for a dangerous mission that was vital to Britain's war effort. When asking what exactly was the mission Cox was told that the operation was still secret and the air commodore was not at liberty to divulge its objectives. Without knowing what was being asked of him, Cox immediately volunteered for the mission and was whisked away to Manchester to undergo parachute training.

C Company exercising their embarkation techniques on one of Dorset's shingle beaches in preparation for the raid. The calm sea and bright sunshine were in stark contrast to many of the previous training sorties, where bad weather and poor organization made them into something of a shambles. Nonetheless, when the time came to put their training into practice during the raid, the paratroopers were embarked with little difficulty once the landing craft had arrived on the beach. (IWM H17407)

When Cox eventually joined up with C Company at its camp at Tilshead he was introduced to Lieutenant Vernon and his sappers along with their NCO, Corporal Jones. Cox was told that he would be working closely with Vernon and six other engineers on the operation to dismantle the German equipment. The flight sergeant was asked to help with the training of the party on the rudiments of radar. Should Cox or Vernon be incapacitated during the raid, it was hoped that at least a few of the other engineers would be able to dismantle something useful from the Würzburg.

An elementary electrical course was run by Lt Vernon to teach the sappers to recognize electrical equipment and to learn how to avoid electrocuting themselves. Later Colonel Schonland, superintendent of the Radar Operational Research Group, gave the engineers lectures on RDF equipment. This included demonstrating with a Mark I Mobile RDF set, which was dismantled and reassembled again and again by the sappers. Finally a test was carried out with a mock-up set made to look as much like the German one as possible. The inside was full of gadgets, some useful, some merely ornamental, to test the sappers' ability to recognize vital equipment.

Lieutenant Vernon and Corporal Jones were also taught the elements of flash photography with a Leica camera to be ready for the task of photographing the German installation. The engineers had duties other than the radar and were taught how to arm and lay Mark IV anti-tank mines along with the use of the recently introduced Polish mine detector. They were also given opportunities to use burglars' tools to open up the set if it was locked – it was later said in a report that the men showed a marked aptitude for this particular task. Training was also given in the use of explosive charges for opening safes etc. In addition to all this work, the sappers joined the paratroopers on the firing range, on map-reading exercises, on night work and on tactical schemes.

Further radar expertise for the raid was to be provided by the addition of a scientist, Donald Priest, from the Telecommunications Research Establishment at Swanage. Priest, however, was a security risk, for he was a leading expert on British radar and familiar with all of the latest developments in RDF. It was imperative that he be kept from any possibility of being made captive. It was therefore decided that Priest would go over to France with the naval force and would wait offshore until word came that Frost's men had totally secured the area, permitting him to land and investigate the whole of the radar site at Bruneval without falling into enemy hands. If the parachutists failed to gain total and complete control of the area then Priest was to remain at sea.

Major John Frost did not join with his company on its move to Tilshead Camp towards the end of January; he had another more pressing task to accomplish. The major had previously been the battalion's adjutant and had taken over C Company only just before word of the special operation arrived. He had not yet completed the statutory number of jumps to acquire his parachute wings, for he had been injured on his first jump the previous year and was unable to return to Ringway aerodrome in Manchester to complete the course.

Whilst his men settled into their new home in draughty barracks on a cold and wintry Salisbury Plain, Frost was trying to squeeze in his last three jumps from Whitley bombers in equally dismal weather in the north of England before the deadline given to him by his colonel expired. Fortunately he made the grade just in time and rushed south to organize his company into a proficient fighting unit before the proposed demonstration to the War Cabinet.

A practice exercise for the company was soon organized on a specially selected area of high ground near Alton Priors close to the Kennet and Avon Canal in Wiltshire. The high ground represented the cliffs at Bruneval and the canal was the sea. The exercise called for C Company to be split into a number of parties, each with a special task and each dropped at small intervals. There were no actual airborne drops to be made during this practice scheme; the purpose of the exercise was to train for the ground operations of the eventual raid.

When the major considered the proposed plan he was not at all happy with it. His company was normally organized into three platoons and a company HQ, and the break-up of this natural formation into fighting groups unbalanced all that the company had previously trained for. He felt sure that the exercise would be a shambles. Frost decided to go to divisional headquarters to see if the organization for the exercise could be changed into something more manageable. There he met with the division's liaison officer, who took the major into his confidence and told him that his company was, in fact, not preparing itself for an important demonstration to members of the War Cabinet, but that this exercise and training on the high ground was a preamble to a raid on enemy territory. The reorganization of Frost's company into small parties was important to the final plan of the operation, as was the addition of the group of Royal Engineers and the tasks set for his company.

The ground training at Alton Priors fortunately turned out to be successful, with all groups accomplishing their tasks to the major's satisfaction, although the whole of this period was often interrupted by heavy snow. On 7 February contact was made with Wing Commander Pickard and his pilots of No. 51 Squadron. The squadron flew Whitley Mark V bombers, which needed some modification to enabled parachutists to exit safely and quickly from the aircraft. The squadron was based at RAF Thruxton for the raid, on an airfield that had just been upgraded to bomber-station standard by the addition of three concrete runways. The aerodrome was located just on the edge of Salisbury Plain, 24km east of Tilshead Camp. It was here that Frost's men practised loading containers and themselves into the aircraft and undertook exit drills. It was also a period during which they could get to know the pilots and their ground crews.

The Armstrong Whitworth Whitley bombers that would take Frost's company to France were, by 1942, coming to the end of their active service. The first prototype twin-engine Whitley had flown in 1936 and was introduced into the RAF the following year, replacing the Handley Page Heyford biplane. When war began it was the oldest of the three bombers in service with the RAF – the other two were the Hampden and the Wellington – and it was by then virtually obsolete, but more than 1,000 of them were produced before a suitable replacement could be put in service. One of its main problems was that it could not maintain altitude on only one engine. The aircraft was designed as a night bomber and flew the first bombing mission against German soil in March 1940. When the need to find a transport aircraft arose from the establishment of parachute forces, the Whitley was selected to temporarily fill the task.

As a transport for airborne troops the Whitley was not the best of aircraft. The only means of exit for the parachutists was through a circular hole cut in its floor. If they did not exit correctly there was a risk they would bang their head against the sides. The inside of the aircraft was very cramped and the troops had to sit on the floor facing alternate ways with their backs against one side and their feet against the other. Loading was crucial to obtain the correct centre of gravity, which was essential for the stability of the aircraft in flight. Each passenger on board had to be weighed along with his weapons and equipment and placed in an appropriate position. Records show that the 12 parachutists in Major

Frost's aircraft weighed 828kg and that Frost himself with his pistol and ammunition weighed 97kg. Such detail was essential for a successful mission.

On 9 February Frost took his men north to Inveraray in Scotland to undertake training with the Royal Navy on Loch Fyne. For five days and nights they practised embarking onto landing craft and moving about the open waters. During this period they stayed on board the Combined Operations support ship *Prinz Albert*, which made a welcome change from the damp conditions at Tilshead Camp. The ship had been built in Belgium in 1937, taken over by the British in 1940, and then armed and converted for use by special forces. The *Prinz Albert* carried eight assault landing craft

This pre-war picture of the tiny beach at Bruneval was used in the planning of Operation *Biting*. It shows just how small a target it was for the landing craft to find on a dark February night. The seafront here is now much changed. (Crown Copyright)

(ALC) and was protected by the addition of a mixture of Oerlikons, 12-pounder and six-pounder guns.

On 14 February C Company returned to Wiltshire ready to participate in practice drills with No. 51 Squadron. The following day there was an airborne drop of the whole force and their containers onto ground close by Major General Browning's HQ at Syrencote House just outside the village of Figheldean, 19km north of Salisbury. Although Frost thought that the exercise was 'a shambles', the general seemed to be satisfied with the drop.

Bad weather continued to interfere with training. A practice with the Royal Navy at Redcliff Point in Dorset was abandoned on 16 February. The next day a full night rehearsal with the landing craft and the RAF was planned to take place in the area of Arish Mell near Lulworth. It was intended that the airborne troops would be lorried to an assembly area as though they had arrived by air and for No. 51 Squadron to drop containers onto the designated drop zone. The troops would rendezvous with their equipment, carry out their set tasks and then withdraw by sea on landing craft. Unfortunately the weather turned bad at the last minute and the landing craft could not arrive. The aircraft dropped the containers wide of their mark and Frost's company went to the wrong place. Major Frost described the exercise as 'a disaster'.

The same was true for the following day at Arish Mell. The landing craft were due to arrive at 2000hrs, but the weather got the better of them and at

A parachutist, wearing the canvas and sorbo-rubber 'bungee' training helmet, is poised to exit through the floor of a Whitley aircraft during parachute training. The picture shows the incredibly cramped conditions inside the aircraft, which could carry no more than 12 troops into battle. (Sgt. Elmer R. Bonter/Dept. of National Defence/Library and Archives Canada/ PA-115854)

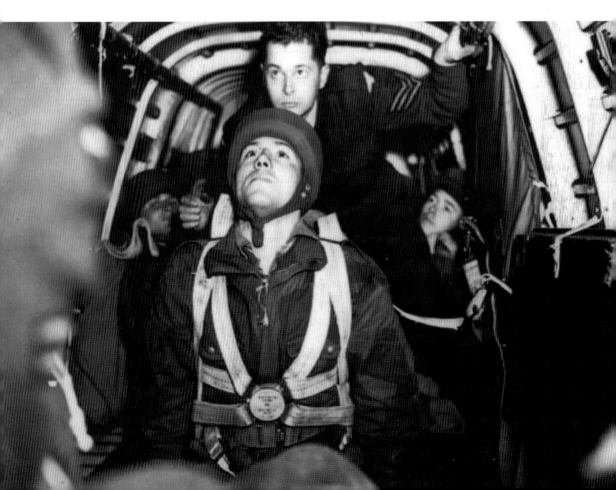

2015hrs the practice was once again called off. The three days spent in Dorset exercising for the raid were a failure. The company returned to Tilshead on 19 February and were told that the operation was set to take place in just five days' time on 24 February. One final attempt to practise with the landing craft took place the next day, 20 February, in Southampton Water. The flat-bottom boats came into the beach as planned at 2015hrs and the troops embarked onto the vessels. However the falling tide left the landing craft stranded in the mud and the troops disembarked and went home to bed.

The RAF had also been busy during this period, preparing No. 51 Squadron for the raid. Group Captain Norman's report after the raid detailed the types of training undertaken by the squadron. First, of course, the pilots had to learn the general theory of dropping parachutists rather than bombs. Next came various familiarization missions such as dropping practice dummies, map-reading at low altitude, timed cross-country flights with low approaches to selected fields, cross-country flights at dusk, a whole-day mission with all 120 paratroopers and a final dusk rehearsal dropping only containers.

Other techniques had to be evolved, one of which was for the automatic release of the equipment containers at the same time as the parachutists. The bomb-release circuit on the Whitley was modified so that its circuitry became active only after the 'green' light for the drop was switched on. The containers were actually released when contact was made via a standard intercom plug. This plug was attached by a short cord to the static strop used by parachutist No. 5. On the 'green' signal the stick of troops would launch themselves from the aircraft, each man's parachute being operated by the static strop. When the No. 5 of the stick jumped out, the static strop freed his parachute and the plug attached to his line then released the containers from the bomb bay allowing the men and their containers to land together.

In addition to providing the 12 Whitley bombers that would fly Major Frost's paratroopers to Bruneval, the RAF had other aspects to their air plan. On several nights prior to the operation, No. 4 Group Bomber Command was to carry out raids with its bombers crossing the coast at low levels close to the objective at Bruneval. This would make the Germans in the area of Le Havre become accustomed to aircraft coming in from the sea at low altitudes. On the night of the operation a diversionary raid was to take place around Le Havre. To protect the sea passage of the naval forces involved in Operation *Biting*, No. 11 Group Fighter Command was to provide fighter cover to the returning ships once daylight had broken. This air cover by Spitfires would escort the small craft all the way back to home waters.

The navy plan was to evacuate and return the raiders to Portsmouth after the operation. Frost's men were to be taken off the beach by landing craft from the vessel *Prinz Albert*. The Combined Operation's ship would leave Portsmouth early on the afternoon of the raid and proceed towards the target area accompanied by Commander Cook's motor gun boats. Off the French coast the *Prinz Albert* would release her landing craft and then return to England, for she was much too big a target to remain at sea in the area throughout the night. The assault landing craft and the MGBs would then close on the beach at Bruneval and await offshore for the signal to run in and pick up the raiders. The paratroopers, including those carrying the vital radar components, would be transferred from the ALCs onto the MGBs which would then tow the landing craft back to the home port (the landing craft themselves did not have the range to return to England under their own power).

The operation was set to take place on the night of 24 February, weather permitting. The last few days before the operation now became filled with activities to perfect the final details. It was a busy period for all involved: equipment had to be collected and tested; special clothing provided; identity discs checked; containers had to be packed; and weapons issued. Further training was undertaken in attacking pillboxes and crossing barbed wire by day and night. Then there was a final rehearsal by each party concentrating on its own particular tasks. Finally, models and air photographs were revealed and each man could at last see the real objectives they would be faced with. The separate groups that had been formed from the start could now learn of their individual targets.

The main object of the raid was to capture various parts of the Würzburg and get them back to England. There were many other secondary objectives to be seized if circumstances permitted. Foremost of these was to capture any German prisoners who might be connected with the radar, especially operators and technicians. Photographs of the whole site were also important, as were any documents and diagrams that might be found at the Würzburg or in the adjacent villa. To complete these tasks the area had to be secured, as did the escape route down to the beach, and the beach itself, to allow the landing craft to come in and embark the paratroopers.

This was to be a lightning raid in which timing was most important. The raiders could not linger too long on their tasks for they were going into action very lightly armed. The payload of the Whitley aircraft was too small to include the carrying of heavy weapons. Frost's men would not have the benefit of mortars or any other means of holding strong enemy forces at bay. The latest light machine pistol, the Sten, was to be the weapon of choice. It had the capability of being very effective at short range – providing it did not jam – and it was light to carry and easy to use. Spraying an area with Sten gunfire was an effective way of making sure the enemy kept his head down. Pistols and rifles were the other weapons to be carried, supplemented by a few Bren light machine-guns. All of these weapons would, however, be ineffective against any armour or mortars that the enemy might bring against them, so the intention was to get in and get out as swiftly as possible.

The final plan called for C Company and its attendant eight Royal Engineers, 120 men in total, to be split into three main groups containing a number of small parties, each of which was allocated a specific task. The parties were each given code names, as were several of the key places within the site to be attacked, the most notable of which was the Würzburg, itself labelled 'Henry'. The names of the individual parties were chosen from a list of notable British admirals and reflected the navy's part in what was a truly combined operation.

'Nelson' was the biggest party, with a particularly vital role to play. It consisted of 40 men organized into three light sections under the command of Lieutenant E. C. B. Charteris and a heavy section led by Captain John Ross, Frost's second-in-command. It was Charteris's objective to capture and hold the beach and to eliminate the fixed enemy positions in the casemates either side of the exit. Captain Ross and his men would provide Charteris with a rearguard as his men moved in to seize these objectives and then seal the road leading from Bruneval village assisted by two sappers with their anti-tank mines. Once these tasks were completed, contact would be made with the naval force and the landing craft could be brought in ready for the evacuation.

The second grouping of paratroopers consisted of three individual parties. 'Drake', with ten men under the command of Lieutenant Peter Naumoff, was charged with containing the enemy housed in the rectangle of buildings at Le Presbytère to the north of the villa. Once the firing began, the first enemy resistance to the landings would most likely come from the coast

Men of C Company practise embarkation drill onto landing craft. During training each group of men was called down to the boats in a strict order, and each craft came in one at a time. During the actual raid, the confusion that surrounded the lateness of the arrival of the landing craft and the eagerness of a radio operator to get the boats to come in immediately meant that all six of them arrived at once and all the men on the beach swarmed forward to be taken off. (IWM 17412)

OPERATION *BITING* COMMANDERS

Commander-in-Chief, Admiral Sir William James, KCB

Admiral William James was born in 1881 and graduated from the naval training ship HMS *Britannia* in 1901. During World War II he served as flag officer on HMS *Benbow* from 1916–17 before joining naval intelligence. He worked as a code breaker in the famous 'Room 40' in Whitehall and eventually became Deputy Director of Naval Intelligence.

Between the wars he served on a number of stations before taking over command of the Battlecruiser Squadron flying his flag in HMS *Hood*. In 1938 he became a full admiral and served as Commander-in-Chief Portsmouth until his retirement from the service in 1944.

Air Force Commander, Group Captain Sir Nigel Norman

Nigel Norman was born in 1897 and served in France during World War I with the Royal Garrison Artillery and Royal Engineers. In 1926 he became a private aircraft owner and joined the Auxiliary Air Service as a pilot officer. In his civilian life he helped form the aviation company Airwork, which specialized in developing airports at home and abroad. He served with No. 601 (County of London) Squadron, where he later acted as a flight commander, and in 1931 he was appointed to command the squadron. He went on to command No. 110 Wing at Ringway and, from 1940, the Central Landing Establishment. His final appointment came in 1942 when he was chosen to form No. 38 Wing. During this time he worked in close collaboration with the army to develop techniques for carrying airborne troops. He was air force commander for the first parachute operation in Italy, then at Bruneval and finally during the invasion of North Africa. Nigel Norman was killed when his aircraft crashed on take-off at Portreath on 19 May 1943.

Naval Force Commander, Commander F. N. Cook RAN

Commander Cook joined the Royal Australian Navy between the wars and was serving in Britain as a lieutenant commander with the Royal Navy when war broke out. He was one of the 375 survivors that escaped from 31,000-ton battleship, HMS *Royal Oak*, when she was sunk in Scapa Flow by Günther Prien's *U-47* on 14 October 1939. He later commanded HMS *Tormentor*, the landing craft operational base at Hamble on Southampton Water. Just after the Bruneval Raid an approach was made to the Royal Navy by the Australian Commonwealth Government seeking advice and assistance in the setting up of a Combined Operations Training Centre at Port Stephens, along the lines of those already operating in England. Commander Cook was assigned to the task and returned to Australia to raise and command the establishment for the remainder of the war.

OC Parachute Troops, Major John Frost

John Frost was one of the most active of all airborne commanders. Of the ten battle honours awarded to the whole of the Parachute Regiment during the war, John Frost fought in four of them: Bruneval, Oudna, Primosole Bridge and Arnhem. He was born in 1912 and after attending the Royal Military Academy Sandhurst was commissioned as a second lieutenant in the Cameronians (Scottish Rifles) in 1932. From 1938 to 1941 Frost was seconded to the Iraq Levies as a captain, where he commanded a force of local tribesmen organized into infantry rifle companies to guard RAF airfields and installations. When he returned to England in 1941 he joined the Parachute Regiment. After the Bruneval Raid he was involved in the Torch landings in North Africa in command of the 2nd Parachute Battalion. He took part in the abortive Oudna operation and then fought his battalion as infantry for the whole of the Tunisian campaign. He led his unit at the Primosole Bridge action in Sicily and in the invasion of Italy. It was, however, in the Arnhem battle that he won his lasting fame, capturing the end of the strategic bridge in the city and holding it for days against overwhelming odds before he and his men capitulated and were made prisoners of war. On release from captivity in 1945, Frost remained in the army and later commanded the 52nd (Lowland) Division. By the time of his retirement from the army in 1968, Frost had attained the rank of major general. He died in 1993.

defence troops and Luftwaffe personnel located there. It was Naumoff's task to protect this northern flank of the area under attack from enemy interference whilst the radar was dismantled. 'Hardy' was commanded by Major Frost himself and his initial objective was to seize and clear the villa. The third party, 'Jellicoe', was led by Lieutenant Peter Young, and its main task was to capture and hold the Würzburg whilst the sappers under Lieutenant Vernon and Sergeant Cox set about dismantling it. The three parties consisted of 30 men in total.

The final group was a single party, 'Rodney', led by Lieutenant John Timothy. Its 40 men would drop last and move to the east of the attack zone to screen off the landward side from any major enemy interference. Timothy's group would also provide a mobile reserve as required and eventually act as a rearguard during the evacuation phase of the raid.

The drop zone for the paratroopers was an area of open ground 365m south-east of the villa. The forming-up point from which each party would launch its attack was a line of trees just to the south-west of the drop zone. Each party would move silently into position and the raid would begin when Major Frost blew his whistle just as his party was launching its attack on the villa. Then the firing would start.

Each group was provided with a No. 38 radio, with all sets working on the same 8MHz frequency operated by company signallers. These sets were intended to be used to co-ordinate the land battle. Regimental signallers

A mobile German Luftwaffe Würzburg radar installation in the field. Unlike the installation at Bruneval the radar operators are open to the elements, for there is no small hut attached to contain the display apparatus. (Bundesarchiv 1011-662-6660-27A)

operated the other communications links that were provided. Two No. 18 sets, working at 8.7MHz, were issued for signalling between the raiding force and the naval craft. To help guide the landing craft into the beach, two systems of homing beacons were provided. The land-based signallers had a portable directional radio transmitter called a 'Rebecca', whilst those in the landing craft used its companion receiver called 'Eureka'. Once the beach was captured the transmitters would be switched on to form an aiming point for the landing craft that would, it was hoped, 'home in' on the right beach in darkness. The system was still in its infancy and the transmitters were fitted with an explosive charge to prevent their capture by the enemy. All four of the regimental signallers operating these sets were to drop with the Rodney group, each man in a separate aircraft.

Operation *Biting* was a raid in which the Royal Engineers took a prominent role. Its main objective was an engineering one and particular care was taken in the planning and training of the objectives that the sappers were to undertake. They were distributed amongst the paratroopers as follows: Nelson: one sergeant and one sapper to lay anti-tank mines and to tape a path through the minefield; Hardy: Lieutenant Vernon, one corporal and one sapper (along with Sergeant Cox of the RAF) to dismantle and photograph the radar set; and Rodney: two sappers to duplicate the work of Nelson if required. To execute these tasks, the engineers had to carry a wide range of tools and equipment including Polish mine detectors, wire-cutters, hammers, jemmies, explosive charges, anti-tank mines, incendiaries, white tape and three trolleys on which to carry away the booty. All these items, plus many others, were to be dropped along with the troops in eight separate containers. Other containers were to be dropped simultaneously containing weapons and equipment for Frost's men. Each of these 12 storage boxes showed a coloured light that illuminated on impact so that every man could quickly recognize those containers relevant to his particular group.

THE RAID

The raid was planned to take place on the night of 24/25 February 1942 and all preparations were geared for this date. The morning of the 24th, the men of C Company checked their weapons, packed their containers and completed all the last-minute tasks that made them ready for action. After lunch the men were told to rest, and grab some sleep if that was possible. After tea, just as they were finally preparing to board trucks for the short journey to Thruxton airfield where No. 51 Squadron's aircraft were waiting for them, news came through from Major General Browning's HQ that the raid had been postponed. Deteriorating weather conditions made it impossible for parachute missions to be flown. The containers were unpacked, weapons shelved and the unit stood down until the next day.

The next morning, 25 February, the paratroopers of C Company went through the same routine of checking and cleaning weapons, packing containers and familiarizing themselves with their tasks, each man once again steeling himself for the forthcoming mission that could be his last. And once again, just after teatime, news came through of another night of buffeting winds and a further postponement.

The following day, 26 February was the last day that the moon and tides would be at their optimum suitability for the attack. Word was that if they did not go that night the raid would have to be cancelled for at least a month. That day all of C Company felt that this had to be the night they had been waiting for. They went through their usual routine with even greater expectation than before, believing that the operation would go ahead even if the weather was going to be slightly chancy. Unfortunately, when it came the news was once again disappointing; the operation was off once more.

On the morning of 27 February Major Frost awoke expecting to receive a message from HQ that his company was to stand down and the men be given leave. Outside, the weather had turned extremely cold, with bright sunshine and a thick frost on the ground. The air was still, with the country sitting under an area of high pressure.

Sixty-four kilometres to the south-east at Portsmouth, Admiral James met with his staff to consider whether they might contemplate carrying out the raid that night, even though the optimum conditions had passed. The calm weather outside and the current forecast indicated that the night might be suitable for airborne operations. The consensus was that the raid should go ahead. Admiral James then spoke with Wing Commander Norman and Major-General Browning to solicit their views and both were willing to give the matter the go-ahead. Browning immediately sent an order to Major Frost for C Company to prepare itself once again for action that night.

On Friday 27 February, for the fourth time that week, Frost's men went through the same routine they had completed many times before. This time there was a difference, for at teatime, just as the men were relaxing after a simple meal, the immaculately dressed Major-General 'Boy' Browning appeared before them at Tilshead Camp to wish them all good luck; the raid was definitely on for that night.

Welsh commandos disembark from a landing craft after their return to England. The commandos went over to France with Commander Cook's flotilla to provide covering Bren gunfire during the embarkation of C Company from the beach at Bruneval. (IWM 17362)

At Portsmouth the decision had been released much earlier, for the navy's part in Operation *Biting* began long before the air and ground forces moved into their start positions. That afternoon the *Prinz Albert*, accompanied by five of Commander Cook's MGBs from the 14th Motor Gun Boat Flotilla and the Hunt Class destroyer HMS *Blencathra*, slipped out of the Solent into the Channel and headed south-east towards the area of sea off France where it would release its landing craft. Although the *Blencathra* would protect the flotilla up to the release point, it would return towards Portsmouth with the *Prinz Albert* after all the small craft were launched from the mother ship. From then on the safety of the tiny convoy would have to rely on the firepower of the sixteen-man MGBs. Each of the craft was armed with two two-pounder guns, two 0.5in machine-guns and one Oerlikon 20mm canon. They also carried two depth charges.

Back at Tilshead Camp trucks came and picked up C Company in the early evening to take them to Thruxton airfield. The men were then housed in three blacked-out Nissen huts around the perimeter whilst they waited for the off. Inside, each of the paratroopers found his parachute suitably packed and lined up along the floor of the building. As the hours before the move ticked by the men ate sandwiches and drank tea, chatting nervously together, checking each other's straps and wishing that they could get the whole thing started. Frost and his officers, accompanied by Company Sergeant-Major Strachan, visited each hut in turn, wishing them good luck and dispensing an air of confidence. They were also told their destination that night, for although they had studied maps and models of the immediate terrain they were to drop into, none knew that their actual destination was an area of France just across the Channel.

Outside one of the huts Group Captain Norman met up with C Company's commander to give him the latest news and to wish him good luck before he left to join Admiral James at Operation *Biting*'s command post in Portsmouth. Newman had just received news from a reconnaissance flight made by a Havoc Mk I of RAF 23 Squadron over the area of Bruneval. Conditions were excellent: the sea very calm, visibility three to six kilometres and cloud cover was 10/10 with a ceiling of 600m. Frost was told there was snow on the ground at Bruneval and that the enemy anti-aircraft fire that night was 'lively'. The major groaned inwardly at the thought of the Germans on the other side of the Channel being alerted by these reconnaissance flights, but was content to hear that his party would be met by snowy ground. Although the snow smocks that had been issued to the unit were left behind at Tilshead Camp, Frost still felt that the snow might be a good thing as it would make things clearer for him to control his men and fight the forthcoming battle.

The time soon came for the parachutists to board the aircraft. When instructed to do so, they cheerfully made their way out onto the apron in parties of ten to board their designated Whitley bomber. An important warning had been included in the operational orders to the troops, which now needed some consideration. To save space, all Elsan lavatories had been removed from the aircraft. 'The troops should relieve themselves last thing before emplaning', stated the instruction. At this last hour, not unexpectedly

**FEBRUARY 27
1942**

**2152hrs
Six assault
landing craft
set out from the
*Prinz Albert***

when considering the amount of tea that had been drunk whilst waiting in the Nissen huts for the order to move to be issued, there was a steady line of men alongside each aircraft watering the fertile soil of Hampshire before they climbed aboard.

In the background Piper Ewan moved around the 12 aircraft playing the regimental marches of the Scottish formations involved in the make-up of the company. Sergeant Cox was reassured by the effect the sound of the pipes had on the Scotsmen: 'bringing them to the boil even though they were excitable enough already', he claimed. Wing Commander Pickard also moved among the aircraft before boarding his Whitley bomber, which would lead the flight. His celebrity status (from his part in the film *Target for Tonight*) and imposing figure helped reassure and inspire those that he met that night.

**FEBRUARY 27
1942**

**2215–2235hrs
The aircraft
carrying
C Company
take off**

The beach at Bruneval today. Changes to the sea defences and modern development have changed the site from its appearance in 1942. (Ken Ford)

38

The Flight

One by one the Rolls-Royce Merlin engines of the bombers coughed into life and gradually warmed up ready for take-off. Inside, the men of C Company were all required to assume an allocated position in the aircraft once they were all on board. They had all been warned, 'for take-off and landing with troops aboard, the pilot will be unable to control the aircraft unless the "take-off position" is correctly taken up. The alternative is a crash', stressed the instruction. Once again, the importance of getting the Whitley's 'centre of gravity' right was being made clear to them

At 2215hrs the lead aircraft took off, followed at regular intervals by the remaining 11 Whitleys. The pilots climbed and trimmed their aircraft for steady flight, whilst the paratroops in the rear settled themselves on the hard ribbed floor of the aircraft struggling to find some way to make themselves more comfortable. For warmth during the flight, each of the troops was issued with an air-force type kapok sleeping bag and a pair of silk gloves to help keep out the cold.

The last of No. 51 Squadron bombers left the ground 18½ minutes after the first. The squadron's initial objective was the coastal departure point above Selsey Bill in Sussex, 88km away to the south-east. With the planes now gone, the work of Ground Controller Thruxton in his control vehicle on the airfield's perimeter was almost complete. All that was now left for Wing Commander Oakley to do was to send the signal 'Walnut Twelve' to C-in-C Portsmouth indicating that all 12 aircraft were airborne and on their way to France.

The road leading from the village of La Poterie to Le Presbytère over which the first German reinforcements moved against the raid. It now has a new name, which reflects the events of 1942 and perpetuates the deeds of the gallant commander of C Company, 2nd Battalion, 1st Parachute Division. (Ken Ford)

Almost an hour earlier, at 2152hrs, out in mid-Channel the crew of the *Prinz Albert* had lowered the last of six assault landing craft into the water. As these small boats pulled away from the mother ship, a lamp flashed out a message of good speed from its bridge. Inside each of the landing craft were four black-faced Welsh commandos, armed and ready with their Bren guns to give supporting fire to the parachutists when the moment for evacuation arrived. The line of small craft, shepherded by their escorting MGBs, then slowly ploughed their way towards the French coast through a crisp cold night, rising and falling on the long slow swell that was blowing through the English Channel. Behind them the *Prinz Albert* and the *Blencathra* steamed a north-westerly course for Selsey Bill, sailing along the route over which Pickard's bombers would fly both to and from their objectives, ready to rescue any aircraft that might have to make a forced landing in the sea.

Wing Commander Pickard in his aircraft MH-B led the flight to the coastal departure point at Selsey Bill arriving dead on schedule. This landmark, close to the radio beacon at RAF Tangmere, was also the rendezvous point for all the aircraft of the squadron. From here the line of

One of the German prisoners captured during the Bruneval operation is brought onto the support ship *Prinz Albert*. It is likely that he was the telephone operator with the beach defences housed in the Villa Stella Maris. (IWM H17354)

12 bombers settled into a long-strung-out formation and fixed course for the planned landfall on the French coast at Fécamp, 16km north of Bruneval. The 12 aircraft flew in three groups of four, with a five-minute separation between the groups.

Across the Channel on the cliff tops above Bruneval, the duty crew of the Würzburg had settled in for another long shift. They had left their billets at Le Presbytère to come on duty at 1900hrs and were set to be relieved at 0800 the next morning. The night watch consisted of eight men, two of whom were on duty on the equipment at a time, whilst the other six slept in the dugout on the site. The operators formerly slept in the villa adjacent to the radar, but some five months previously in September 1941 the villa had been hit by incendiary bombs, one of which fell on the Feldwebel's bed, and the crew thereafter decided that the dugout was preferable. Each of the men on duty would spend 97 minutes at the apparatus, with 98 minutes on guard in the lookout post. The lookout post was some distance from the radar and consisted of a hole 90cm square containing binoculars, a machine-gun and a telephone with a direct line to a coast defence reporting centre near Le Havre.

The Whitleys flew through the dark night at a steady 200kph, making the journey seem interminable to the men crouched inside the aircraft in their sleeping bags. Gradually the enemy coast came into view out of the gloom and ten minutes before making landfall the pilots of each aircraft alerted the parachutists in their rear. 'Prepare for action' was shouted down the aircraft to each man in turn above the steady drone of the engines. Inside the belly of the bombers men began struggling out of their sleeping bags and fixing their static lines from their parachutes to the fastening wire that ran down the length of the aircraft.

Eighty kilometres away to the south-west, Havocs of No. 23 Squadron were stirring up the German air defences around Le Havre. They were carrying out a diversionary attack on an aerodrome and railway marshalling yard south-east of the port. The whole area went on to full alert as the enemy expected the attack to develop into a heavy British bombing raid and the sky became lit up with wavy lines of tracer fire and searchlights, clearly visible to the flotilla of small craft heading for Bruneval.

Just before reaching Fécamp, the first group of aircraft banked to starboard and began flying southwards parallel to the coast, about 800m out to sea. Their pilots began identifying landmarks as they went in order to give themselves an accurate fix on their position. The first two aircraft made the manoeuvre without incident, but all of the following aircraft ran into anti-aircraft fire from flak ships anchored off Yport and gun emplacements at Saint-Jouin-sur-Mer. The fire aimed at the low-flying Whitleys was fairly accurate and three of the aircraft took hits, although no great damage was done to any of them. There were no casualties.

The lead aircraft were now flying at between 300 and 450m and soon passed the promontories at Vattetot and Etretat, then the lighthouse at Cap d'Antifer and finally came alongside the clear rectangle of trees and buildings at Le Presbytère just north of the drop zone. This was the signal for 'action stations' to be sounded to the parachutists. In each aircraft the cover was now taken off the exit hole that had been cut in the floor of the bomber and the men inside were able to see the calm moonlit sea slipping by below them. A cold rush of air swept into the aircraft, which made each man shiver and stiffen his resolve to be out into the dark sky amongst the business of the night.

Much earlier the Freya radar station just to the north of the Bruneval Würzburg had picked up the incoming bombers. The operators reported aircraft to the NNE at a range of 75km. The range and bearing of the intruders was passed to the Würzburg as the aircraft closed on the coastline. At around 60km the Würzburg had gone into action and the whole crew alerted to tune their aerial towards the enemy aircraft, but first the apparatus had to be switched on and calibrated – the cathode ray tube display itself took two minutes to become operational. Once the set was working the operator had to regulate the apparatus by pointing the aerial towards some object that would reflect a known steady blip. In this case he swung the parabaloid to a bearing of 45° towards Etretat and a well-known local echo 17km away.

When the radar was satisfactorily calibrated the operator traversed the radar aerial onto the bearing indicated by the Freya station through his loudspeaker. Soon the raiders came up on the Bruneval screen and the Luftwaffe signaller locked on to the path of the intruders by turning handles to control the lateral movement and elevation of the parabaloid. When the maximum blip was seen on his screen he reported his contact to

One of the photographs used in the planning of the raid, made available to all who took part in the operation. It shows the area around the radar site. In the centre of the picture is the villa, with the rectangle of woods at Le Presbytère just above. The dotted line shows the path of the transport aircraft over the landing ground, with the red 'X' showing the point at which the 'red for get ready' light showed in the aircraft, and the green 'X' the point where the 'green for go' lamp illuminated. (Crown Copyright)

his HQ by telephone, first giving his post number, W110. His first report at 2355hrs relayed the range and bearing of the aircraft when they were 29km away and he continually updated this data to HQ at 3km intervals. The targets were moving relatively slowly and were undoubtedly a bomber force. He watched carefully as he saw the intruders reach the area of Fécamp 16km to the north and then, to his alarm, the aircraft turned south and proceeded down the coast heading straight for the radar site. Alarm bells rang and the warnings were flashed around; the station was about to be bombed! There was a mad rush for the shelter.

Down on the beach, in the large empty villa called Stella Maris, the non-commissioned officer (NCO) in charge of the beach defences was awakening those of his men who were asleep, ordering them to put on their equipment and take their turn on guard. One, who was later destined to become a

**FEBRUARY 28
1942**

**0013–0030hrs
The
parachutists land
at Bruneval**

EVENTS

1 Early afternoon, 27th February. The Combined Operations Support Ship *Prinz Albert*, the escort destroyer HMS *Blencathra*, and Commander Cook's flotilla of MGBs leave Portsmouth for France at the start of Operation Biting

2 2152 hours, 27th February. Landing craft leave *Prinz Albert* and head for the waters off Bruneval beach.

3 2215 hours, 27th February. The Whitley aircraft of 51 Squadron take off from Thruxton airfield in Hampshire with Major Frost's company of paratroopers and head for Bruneval.

4 0015 hours, 28th February. 51 Squadron drops the first of C Company's parachutists on Bruneval at the start of the raid.

5 0315 hours, 28th February. The last of the landing craft leave Bruneval beach with Major Frost's paratroopers at the end of the raid.

6 0800 hours, 28th February. A fighter escort of Spitfires from 11 Group provides an air umbrella for the journey back to Portsmouth.

7 0825 hours, 28th February. Destroyer escort rendezvous with Commander Cook's flotilla for the journey back to Portsmouth.

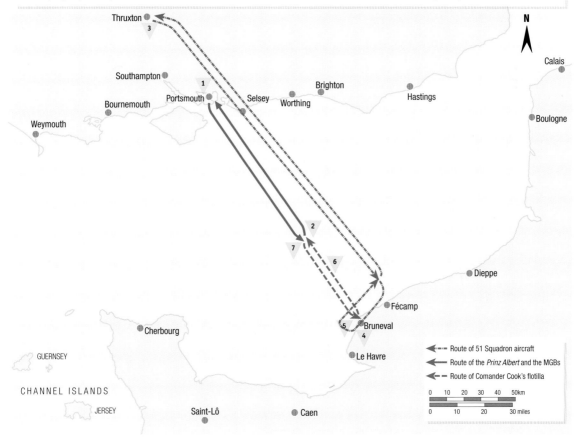

prisoner of the raiders, recalled that he had been sleeping after he had come off duty at around 2110 the previous evening. Just a telephone operator had remained awake in the villa. The NCO rebuked his men for being slow to get ready and then went outside. He could hear the sound of low-flying aircraft.

Gradually the aircraft lost height until they were 5km south of the objective, where they turned 180° to port to begin the final run into the drop zone. They now flew 450m inshore and parallel to the line of cliffs, heading north-eastwards towards Bruneval. At a height of 100m they flew straight and level, ready to release their passengers. As they passed over the road leading from the village of Bruneval to the beach the red 'get ready' light above the trapdoor in the aircraft went on. A few seconds later, when the planes were above the forming-up point on the south of the drop zone, on went the green 'go' light and out of the floor of the aircraft at a fast regular pace the first of the 120 parachutists began their descent. The lead aircraft had arrived at the drop zone 75 seconds earlier than scheduled at just after 0013hrs, with the following Whitley releasing its load 45 seconds earlier than planned. The remaining two bombers of the group arrived dead on the target time of 0015hrs. However the pilot of MH-T, flying at the rear of the group, was slightly wayward with his ground recognition and released Lieutenant Charteris and his stick on the area of high ground 160m to the south of Bruneval village.

With their passengers released safely onto the dark snow-covered landscape, the first four aircraft increased speed and altitude and flew north parallel to the coast for 16km before turning to port to set course for the radio beacon at Tangmere and home. Pickard was pleased that the first two

The site of the villa and Würzburg radar at Bruneval today. After the raid the Würzburg was moved into the Freya compound and the area fortified by a ring of gun emplacements and bunkers. These were blown up at the end of the war and remain in a derelict condition on what is now private land. (Ken Ford)

aircraft of the squadron had experienced no enemy interference from either flak ships or from anti-aircraft positions near Saint-Jouin-sur-Mer, which suggested that no hostile action had been expected by the enemy. It looked as though Operation *Biting* had achieved total surprise.

Five minutes after the lead group had dropped its cargoes, the second group of aircraft came in. They were one Whitley short, for the pilot of MH-Q had not been sure of his position approaching Fécamp and had made a dummy run down the coast until he had established his bearings, a manoeuvre that put him 19 minutes late over the target. The remaining three aircraft arrived over the drop zone on time at 0020hrs.

The last group to arrive experienced one or two problems. The first aircraft reached the drop zone a minute early at 0024hrs. The second Whitley mistook the target and dropped his stick short of Bruneval. The third bomber, MH-X, was at target on time, at 0025hrs, but the fifth man in the stick got hung up and prevented anyone following him out through the exit. The unfortunate individual was quickly hauled back into the aircraft, but by then the plane was well past the drop zone and unable to release any more men. Undaunted, the pilot banked to port and flew out to sea to line himself up for another attempt. He came into the target once again five minutes later at 0030hrs and successfully dropped the remainder of the stick. The fourth aircraft of this third group had meanwhile succeeded with his drop at 0026hrs.

Mission accomplished, all of the aircraft set course for England. The first one landed back at Thruxton at 0140hrs and the last about 50 minutes later. Of the three damaged Whitleys, one had been hit in the main spar by a cannon shell, one had minor damage to the fabric of the body of the aircraft and the other had been hit in the rear turret. As soon as Wing Commander Pickard had made his report and been debriefed, he took a short rest and then rushed down to Operation *Biting*'s command post at Portsmouth. He wanted news of the raid and to be there in the port to see the arrival of Frost's men when they returned home.

The Attack

With the green light glowing above his head and the voice of the dispatcher ringing in his ear, Major Frost launched himself through the hole in the belly of the Whitley and out into the dark night. A great jolt pulled his body upwards as his parachute deployed and for several brief seconds he drifted gently down to earth. For a moment he could see laid below him all the landmarks around the drop zone that he had memorized from maps and models during training. Everything looked perfect in the moonlight. He was delighted as he realized that he and his men had been dropped right on target, but was uncomfortable with the full bladder he had been nursing during the past hour in the aircraft. He couldn't wait to relieve himself of all the liquid he had drunk before departure and cursed himself inwardly for doing so.

Frost landed softly in about 30cm of snow and immediately set about relieving himself, as did many of his stick who were then landing silently

OPERATION *BITING* – THE ATTACK

0013HRS, 28 FEBRUARY 1942

The opening moves of Operation *Biting* began when the first of C Company's parachutists dropped out of the lead Whitley bomber and drifted silently down onto the landing zone just a few hundred metres from the Würzburg radar. The remainder of the 12-man stick followed closely behind. Surprise was complete for no enemy fire met their descent.

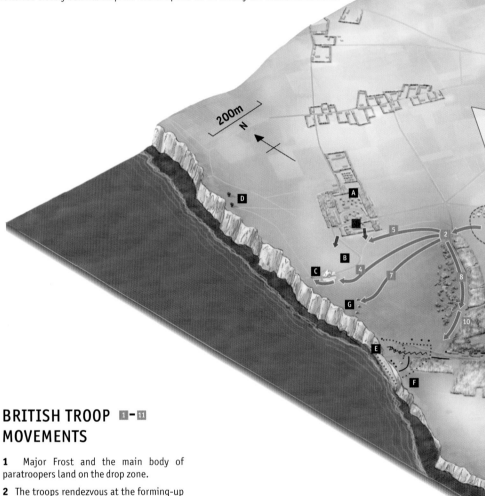

BRITISH TROOP ❶-⓫ MOVEMENTS

1 Major Frost and the main body of paratroopers land on the drop zone.

2 The troops rendezvous at the forming-up point.

3 Lieutenant Charteris and two sticks of paratroopers from Nelson group land 3.2km short of the drop zone.

4 Major Frost with the Hardy and Jellicoe groups moves off to attack 'Lone House' and 'Henry'.

5 Lieutenant Naumoff and Drake group advance to secure the northern perimeter of the airborne lodgement.

6 Lieutenant Timothy and Rodney group move eastwards to protect a landward screen.

7 A small section from Nelson group moves across from forming-up point to attack the three casemates on the northern cliff.

8 Captain Ross and the remainder of Nelson group move down gully to attack the main German positions guarding the beach road.

9 Lieutenant Charteris moves north with his wayward paratroopers to join in the attack to clear the beach.

10 Captain Ross' advance down the gulley is halted by opposition from the German defences on the south cliff.

11 Lieutenant Charteris' group moves through Bruneval to attack and secure the beach, assisted by Captain Ross and his men.

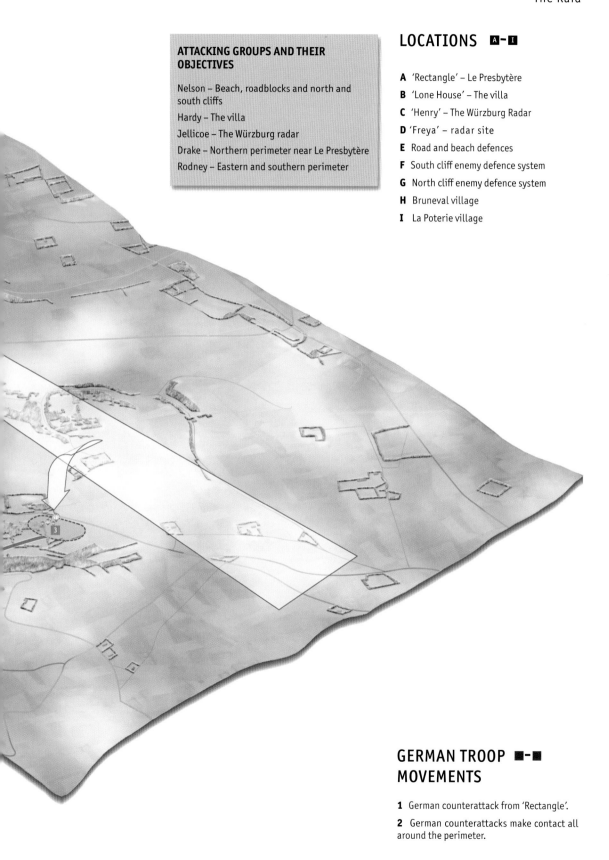

ATTACKING GROUPS AND THEIR OBJECTIVES

Nelson – Beach, roadblocks and north and south cliffs

Hardy – The villa

Jellicoe – The Würzburg radar

Drake – Northern perimeter near Le Presbytère

Rodney – Eastern and southern perimeter

LOCATIONS A–I

A 'Rectangle' – Le Presbytère
B 'Lone House' – The villa
C 'Henry' – The Würzburg Radar
D 'Freya' – radar site
E Road and beach defences
F South cliff enemy defence system
G North cliff enemy defence system
H Bruneval village
I La Poterie village

GERMAN TROOP MOVEMENTS ■–■

1 German counterattack from 'Rectangle'.

2 German counterattacks make contact all around the perimeter.

A post-raid Tobruk machine-gun post looks out across the drop zone from a position near the site of the villa. (Ken Ford)

about him. Above them the sound of the aircraft engines gradually faded into the distance, leaving the area in silence. The first task was to gather weapons and equipment from the appropriate containers scattered about and to move to the rendezvous point along a line of trees a few hundred metres away to the south-west. As they were doing so the second group of aircraft came in low overhead and dropped their passengers. Everything seemed to be going according to plan, with no enemy reception party waiting for their arrival. There was some fire coming from the area around the Freya radar site to the north, but this seemed to be aimed at the retreating aircraft. The enemy in the Würzburg site must know that they were there, for they would have certainly tracked the aircraft down over the cliffs, but for the moment they were silent.

A short time later at the forming-up point Frost learned that two of the light sections of the Nelson group and Lieutenant Charteris had not arrived. This was a blow for the major, for Charteris's three sections had the important task of capturing the beach exit and the German defences on either side to open the way down to the sea. Frost asked Captain Ross to wait a few more minutes for the missing men and then take his heavy section to try to open the road leading down from Bruneval to the beach exit. The one remaining light section should then move to tackle the pillboxes on the northern cliffs below the radar. The capture of these three emplacements was of vital importance, for they barred the planned withdrawal route from the radar site down to sea level. On a brighter note, Lieutenant Timothy and his Rodney group had, for the most part, arrived and were starting to disperse to form the inland screen around the landings.

The drop had been watched by both the German Army and the Luftwaffe. The troops defending the Freya site and the Luftwaffe personnel garrisoned in Le Presbytère had been roused by the alarm and by the low-flying aircraft passing overhead. At 0015hrs a message was sent to First Company, 685th Infantry Regiment at Le Poterie explaining that parachutists had been sighted. This company was part of the defence force responsible for both the radar installations and that section of the coast. Based inland just under 5km from the sea with little transport of its own, its troops had to march into position.

The company was located to provide the first reinforcements against any incident notified by those men on duty on the coast.

By chance, the German company in La Poterie had one of its platoons out on exercise that night and these troops had just returned to the village. The company commander now sent them straight on to Le Presbytère and also alerted the Bruneval Guard that something was afoot, but the sergeant in charge in the village was already well aware that the British had landed just to the north of him. He was now ordered to occupy the defences in the village and on the high ground behind the beach exit with a platoon of men to prevent the British moving down to the beach and to guard against any landings from the sea. Down on the beach itself the NCO on duty there was called to the telephone and told by Company HQ that troops had landed on the high ground a little inland. The NCO ordered the light machine-gun to be brought from the post covering the beach to the villa together with one of the men who was guarding the seafront. The NCO then assembled his section ready to bar the way down to the sea from the high ground to the north on which the British had landed.

When Sergeant Cox had landed he'd joined up with two sappers to search for the containers showing purple lights, which indicated they contained engineering stores, and for the trolleys, which were lodged in containers lit by yellow lights. Once they had found their equipment, they immediately extinguished the lights in order not to become a target for enemy snipers, and dragged the equipment towards the rendezvous point. By this time Lieutenant Drake was also down together with his NCO Corporal Jones. 'We found the containers,' he later wrote, 'and started to unstrip the trolley. I left Jones to complete the job and I went over the crest of the hill to the forming-up point to collect the rest of the sappers. I waited between five and ten minutes for the other sapper detachments to reach the place that I had appointed to meet them, and they brought with them a trolley and a box of tools for doing the job.'

Frost now believed that things were sufficiently under control for the main tasks to be set in motion. He and Lieutenant Young now set off towards the villa and the radar site with the Hardy and Jellicoe groups, whilst Lieutenant Naumoff and his Drake group moved to the north to deal with the expected resistance and possible counterattack that would come from the German troops in Le Presbytère. The area was still remarkably silent. At the same time Lieutenant Vernon and his group set off towards the radar site, pulling their three trolleys across the snow. They moved well to the left of the major, following the edge of the hill overlooking the valley that carried the road. After about 180m Vernon ordered Cox and three sappers to stay with the trolleys as he moved up towards the objective with the other two sappers, explaining he would send a message for them to come up when the area had been cleared.

Major Frost and Lieutenant Young led their men quietly over the snow towards their objectives 550m away. As they neared the villa, Frost sent Young's party away to the left to close on the Würzburg site. 'According to plan,' Frost was to later write, 'silently and stealthily we surrounded the villa,

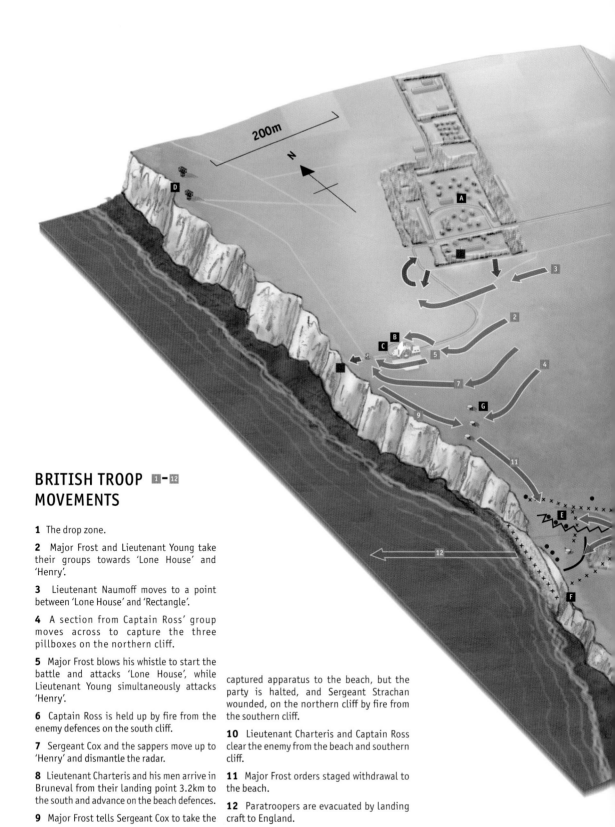

BRITISH TROOP MOVEMENTS 1-12

1 The drop zone.

2 Major Frost and Lieutenant Young take their groups towards 'Lone House' and 'Henry'.

3 Lieutenant Naumoff moves to a point between 'Lone House' and 'Rectangle'.

4 A section from Captain Ross' group moves across to capture the three pillboxes on the northern cliff.

5 Major Frost blows his whistle to start the battle and attacks 'Lone House', while Lieutenant Young simultaneously attacks 'Henry'.

6 Captain Ross is held up by fire from the enemy defences on the south cliff.

7 Sergeant Cox and the sappers move up to 'Henry' and dismantle the radar.

8 Lieutenant Charteris and his men arrive in Bruneval from their landing point 3.2km to the south and advance on the beach defences.

9 Major Frost tells Sergeant Cox to take the captured apparatus to the beach, but the party is halted, and Sergeant Strachan wounded, on the northern cliff by fire from the southern cliff.

10 Lieutenant Charteris and Captain Ross clear the enemy from the beach and southern cliff.

11 Major Frost orders staged withdrawal to the beach.

12 Paratroopers are evacuated by landing craft to England.

OPERATION *BITING* – THE WITHDRAWAL

0315HRS, 28 FEBRUARY 1942

The last landing craft leaves Bruneval with C Company's rearguard. Although the main parts of the Würzburg radar had been stripped and packed away during the first hour, it took two more hours of fighting, reorganizing and nervous waiting before the attack phase of Operation *Biting* was finally brought to a close. Stiff enemy opposition and signalling failures delayed the raiders' attempts to make a swift embarkation from the beach.

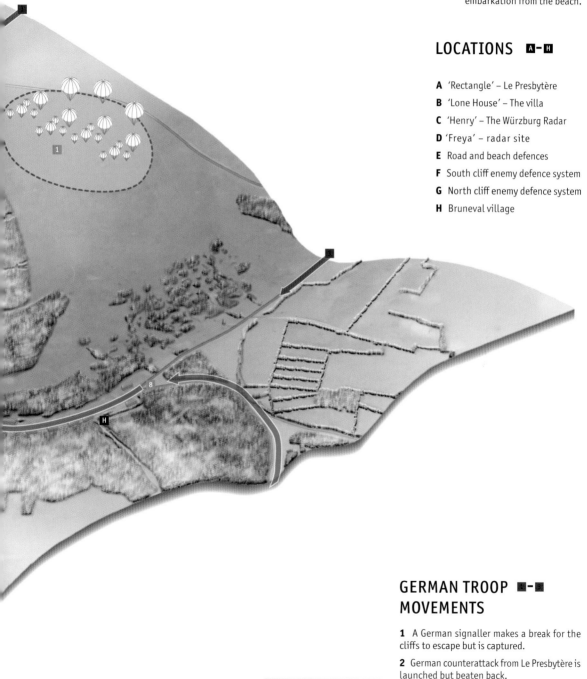

LOCATIONS A–H

A 'Rectangle' – Le Presbytère
B 'Lone House' – The villa
C 'Henry' – The Würzburg Radar
D 'Freya' – radar site
E Road and beach defences
F South cliff enemy defence system
G North cliff enemy defence system
H Bruneval village

GERMAN TROOP MOVEMENTS 1–3

1 A German signaller makes a break for the cliffs to escape but is captured.

2 German counterattack from Le Presbytère is launched but beaten back.

3 German counterattacks from La Poterie make contact with the British perimeter.

Machine-gun post

and when everybody was in position I walked to the door.' He could see that Young's party was in position at the radar site ready for the signal. The door was wide open and the major walked through it remembering only at the last minute to blow his whistle. Then all hell seemed to break loose.

Frost and his men burst through the downstairs rooms throwing grenades and sweeping the area with Sten gunfire. The whole building was empty, but above the noise of the battle outside at the radar pit Frost could hear firing coming from above. The paratroopers rushed up the stairs and surprised a lone German who was firing down on Young's party. He was killed by a burst of Sten. The rest of the house was searched and found to be completely empty of people and furniture.

Outside, the battle around the Würzburg was rather one-sided; so complete was the surprise of the attack that Lieutenant Young had almost reached his objective before encountering any opposition. The German sentry challenged the approaching troops twice and then fired. The paratroops, who had up until then been holding their fire as long as possible, shot him dead. 'After that,' recalled Lieutenant Young later, 'we hunted them out of cellars, trenches and rooms with hand grenades, automatic weapons, revolvers and knives. Most were killed, but some ran away, and one tried to hide over the edge of the cliff. Having got there, he wanted to surrender, and I looked over to see him with his hands up. At the time I thought I had seen nothing funnier than a German trying to scramble up the lip of a cliff with his hands up.'

The German was pulled back up the cliff face and frogmarched over to Frost and Private Newmann, the interpreter. Newmann looked at the prisoner and then reached over and tore the swastika badge from his uniform. 'Why did you do that?' someone asked. 'For my personal satisfaction', smiled the German-born Jew. Frost told Newmann to get what information he could from the German. The frightened captive readily admitted that he was from the Luftwaffe Communications Regiment and was a radar operator. He was just the sort of prisoner that Frost was looking to take home with him.

'I started to interrogate the prisoner about the number of German troops and their positions – we only had some information till then – and I thought he was lying', recalled Private Newmann later. 'So I shook him by his lapels and said so, and my comrade said we should kill him. But I said no as we had to have prisoners and he was very young and started to cry and was shaking with fear, so I said we should take him along. And we did.'

During the interrogation Frost learned from the prisoner that there were about 100 Luftwaffe personnel up at Le Presbytère, who were fully armed to act as a defence for the site. The nearby village of Bruneval was said to be garrisoned by a company of infantry.

The sound of fighting at the villa stirred everyone into action, including the enemy. The Germans housed in the rectangle of trees and buildings that made up Le Presbytère started to react to the British raid with small-arms fire. This fire increased when the first platoon of reinforcements arrived from La Poterie. Lieutenant Naumoff and his men returned this fire from positions in the open between the enemy and the villa. Major Frost now sent word for Vernon, Cox and the sappers to come forward to deal with the Würzburg whilst his and Lieutenant Young's detachments dealt with the opposition to the north. Two men were left to occupy the villa and the others moved out to counter the enemy. It was now that the raid suffered its first fatality when Private McIntyre was hit by small-arms fire as he came out of the house.

In the meantime, Lieutenant Vernon and his sappers had taken a wide route up to the radar, which took them past the machine-gun posts along the cliff. Fortunately these proved to be empty and they carried on to join the men at the Würzburg. 'I met up with Lieutenant Young at 0050hrs at the equipment,' later recorded Vernon, 'and asked him to give me the latest information about what he had seen and done. He told me he had examined the square dugouts up on the cliff edge and found some optical range-finding instruments in there but no radiolocation equipment. He had also examined the dugout a few yards from the radar and had shot a German coming out. In addition, he had been in the house and found no equipment or papers of any kind. There were no signs of occupation except in one room which was used as a billet.'

The area around the objective was now clear and word was sent back for Cox and the remainder of the sappers to come forward with the tools and the trolleys. The sergeant had been waiting behind a small ridge for the call to move forward and when he and the sappers did so they found it difficult

Squadron Leader Pickard, commanding officer of RAF No. 51 Squadron, which took the paratroopers to France, talks with some of the raiders on their return to Portsmouth. They are inspecting a German helmet, a trophy seized during the operation. (IWM H17347)

The rectangle of woods that surrounds the buildings of Le Presbytère as seen from just to the right of the site of the villa. It was across this ground that the first German counterattack against the raiders was launched by coast defence and Luftwaffe troops. (Ken Ford)

to drag the trolleys uphill through the snow. When they got within 45m of the radar they met the low belt of barbed wire that surrounded the installation. 'It was not more than two feet [61cm] high,' recalled Cox later, 'a criss-cross network about ten feet [3m] thick. In view of the obstacle it would have been better to have made arrangements for carrying the equipment and tools, etc. in haversacks rather than trolleys.'

Cox met with Vernon and the officer gave him a brief summary of what he had found on the site. The Würzburg radar installation consisted of a large parabolic aerial, perhaps 3m across. It was mounted on a chassis with a large box containing electrical equipment attached at the rear. Alongside this, also mounted on the chassis, was the small hut used the by the German signallers when operating the radar. A short distance away was a half-buried personnel shelter heaped over with earth and just outside the barbed-wire ring was a storage shelter. The area was now secure, but enemy opposition from the rectangle of buildings of the Freya site was becoming troublesome. Work could now begin on the main objective of the raid.

On the other side of the valley behind the cliffs to the south, Lieutenant Charteris and his men had landed in open fields 3km short of the drop zone. The young lieutenant was only 20, the youngest officer of the force, and therefore known as 'Junior'. He now had to find his way back to the rest of the company through an area quite unknown to him. When Junior took his first look around and failed to recognize any familiar landmark he knew he was lost. He later described his feelings to a newspaper reporter: 'I don't think there's any feeling quite so unpleasant as suddenly finding yourself in enemy territory and not knowing where you are', he said. 'Then I saw another plane going along low down and I knew in which direction to go, and after a while I saw the lighthouse. Then everything was all right.'

His task was to capture the beach exit and help eliminate the enemy from positions on either side, but he now had the added problem of reaching his objective along a route that he had not planned for. When his men hit the ground they began the actions they had trained for. They located the containers with their weapons and explosives and assembled with Charteris to receive orders and some indication of how they would reach their objective.

Whilst the rendezvous was taking place, Lieutenant Charteris dispatched two scouts to reconnoitre the area. The group had landed in the Val aux Chats close by the small village of l'Enfer and the scouts reported back that there was a narrow road to the north-west that led down to Bruneval village. Charteris realized that the only way of reaching the beach exit in time to carry out his objective was if he used that road, even though it led straight into the area that was known to garrison a company of German infantry.

The lieutenant set his men off at a jog, leading them as quietly as possible down the narrow track. The soft snow padded the noise of their boots and they almost reached the village before any sign of the enemy was seen. Charteris decided to go as far as he could before opening fire and alerting the Germans. Just outside Bruneval the party moved off the road to the right to skirt behind the houses on the northern side of the road that led into the village from the east. A few of the enemy were seen and one unfortunate German joined the party thinking that he was with friendly troops, only to be dispatched silently with a commando knife.

Captain Ross had been waiting for some time for news of Charteris's party and when firing was heard from the north he knew Major Frost had begun his attack on the villa. Ross now began to implement an improvised scheme to capture the area around the beach exit. The initial plan drawn up before the raid was that there would be an assault from three sides. One section would attack the three casemates on the northern cliff that barred the route down from the radar site to sea level. A second assault, led by Lieutenant Charteris himself, would attack from the south against the defences around the pillbox and trenches above the Villa Stella Maris on the other side of the exit. These two attacks would then clear the enemy right down to the beach. A third light section would work its way down towards the beach in the centre as far as the wire barricade and give supporting fire as the other assaults went in. Captain Ross and his heavy section would form a block against interference from the German infantry in the village.

Captain Ross now had to achieve these same tasks with much fewer men. He decided that his two remaining light sections would carry out two of the assaults as planned: Sergeant Tasker would take his section to attack the German casemates on the cliff between the radar site and the beach, whilst Sergeant Sharp worked his way down to the wire in front of the beach exit. Ross himself would lead the remainder of his heavy section down the narrow tree-covered ravine that led to the beach road and try to perhaps work his way across to the other cliff overlooking the beach. He intended to reach a position from which he could clear the enemy from the defences behind Stella Maris as best he could. Unless the whole area near the beach was cleared and held, there would be no evacuation for anyone that night. There was one comforting thought though: Lieutenant Timothy and his inland screen was dispersed a few hundred metres behind him, holding back any enemy reinforcements that might arrive. In the meantime he and his men would have to deal with the Germans that were already there in the village.

The attack began well with both sergeants advancing carefully on their objectives, Tasker stalking the casemates whilst Sharp infiltrated down to the wire perimeter. Captain Ross did not get too far before his group was spotted by the enemy. Across the other side of the road the German NCO covering the beach section had spotted men moving down the gulley. In order to satisfy himself that they were not Germans he fired a white flare into the sky, bathing the area in brilliant light. When he received no answering signal he fired his machine pistol high in the air in that direction. By then he was convinced that the troops were British and got his men up onto the high ground behind the villa to engage the enemy. Ross and his men returned this fire but became pinned down for a while, finding it difficult to move.

Back at the radar site Frost learned that there was still no sign of Lieutenant Charteris and his men. With the radar taken, the most

Two of the three German prisoners are brought on board the support ship *Prinz Albert* moored just off Portsmouth. Each is being searched by paratroopers before being handed over to army troops. The prisoner on the right is the Luftwaffe radar operator captured after trying to escape over the cliff. Interesting to note is the right breast of his torn tunic. It is missing the Nazi Luftwaffe badge, which was torn away by Private Newmann, the German-born Jewish interpreter. The paratrooper on the left carries his own rifle and a German one; a trophy from the raid. (IWM 17353)

important task facing the major now was to seize the escape route to the beach. He knew that Captain Ross's group was 20 men short and needed some assistance to ensure success. Frost decided to reinforce Ross with Lieutenant Naumoff's party, who were at that moment shielding the villa and radar site from those of the enemy in Le Presbytère. Naumoff's task would be taken over by some of Lieutenant Timothy's men who were holding the landward flank, supported by Frost himself and the men who were with him.

Out at sea the tiny flotilla of small craft poised to rescue the parachutists had reached the area off Bruneval and were waiting for the signal to come in to the beach. The weather was changing and the still air was gradually giving way to a freshening wind. While they waited, a line of larger ships came into view a 1.6km or so farther out to sea. Two German destroyers and two E-boats, sufficiently powerful a force to have wiped out the British craft, were steaming quite fast from east to west, seemingly heading for Le Havre. Fortunately the landing craft and MGBs were low in the water against a dark shore and were not seen by the enemy ships but, just after they had moved off and the danger was over, the white flare fired by the German defenders near the beach went up. A few moments earlier and the airborne illumination would have placed Commander Cook's flotilla in silhouette against its bright light.

Whilst all this noise of battle echoed back and forth across the cliff tops, Lieutenant Vernon and Sergeant Cox began the main work of the night, the stealing of Hitler's radar secrets. Cox confronted the very thing that had dominated his thoughts for the past few weeks, the Würzburg. 'I surveyed the apparatus,' he was later to write, 'and found it to my surprise just like the photographs. The first point of interest was the aerial, which I looked at, and one of the sappers proceeded to cut it from the centre. I went round the back tracing the aerial lead to the top box of the parabaloid.' Here the sergeant found a strong metal box that contained three smaller boxes. The largest of these contained the transmitter, local oscillator and mixer; the one below on the left was the IF amplifier and the other the pulse generator. All three of these boxes contained the bulk of the material Cox and Vernon were looking for.

Cox and Corporal Jones now began working to remove this apparatus from the metal chassis of the box with screwdrivers whilst Vernon supervised the removal of the aerial and began photographing the installation. The first of the flashes seemed to attract a great deal of fire from the enemy and bullets started to ping off the front of the parabaloid. The party was coming under increasing attention from the rectangle to the north, as were those troops defending the area between Le Presbytère and the villa. The enemy was becoming bolder, shifting position and moving out of the confines of trees and buildings into more open ground.

Cox and Jones were finding it almost impossible to remove any of the boxes by conventional means; the finely engineered equipment was reluctant to come clear through the use of just screwdrivers and spanners. In the end, with gunfire echoing all around and the other paratroopers getting impatient

OVERLEAF
The whole point of Operation *Biting* was the capture of as much equipment from the Würzburg radar installation as was feasible and it was the presence of a party of men from the Royal Engineers with the attack group that made this possible. The scene shows the RAF technician Sergeant Cox and sapper Corporal Jones using brute force to free parts of the apparatus after a more refined approach using spanners and screwdrivers had failed. They worked as fast as they could, for timing was most important. The radar was very exposed and all the while that the sappers were engaged in their work the enemy tried to interfere with carefully aimed small arms fire. It was fortunate that none of these specialists were killed or injured during the operation.

to leave, the two men resorted to brute force. 'During the whole period of working at the equipment, bullets were flying much too close to be pleasant, but while we were working at the back of the dish we were protected by the metal of the parabaloid itself', recalled Cox later. He and Corporal Jones decided to rip the rest of the apparatus out using hammer, chisel and jemmy, even if this meant breaking a few things in the process.

Lieutenant Vernon had noticed that there were some signs on the inside of the parabaloid aerial. He counted 57 markings against an outline of a plane and two against a design of a ship. Later study indicated that these were most likely the number of 'kills' attributed to the installation, although probably exaggerated. Vernon managed to take just a few pictures before he was forced to stop photographing by enemy fire. Those few pictures were of poor quality and of little use to the scientists. The lieutenant did manage to look inside the operator's hut attached to the Würzburg, but had little time to remove anything. Nonetheless, his later description of the equipment inside was of great use to the experts back in England. The most important piece of apparatus inside the cabin was the unit containing the cathode ray tube on which the information gained by the radar was displayed to the operator. It was not possible to remove anything from the cabin because at that moment time had started to run out for the raiders. The Germans had become emboldened and were pressing hard against the northern perimeter of the lodgement.

As Cox had observed earlier, the paratroops around the radar and the villa were now getting impatient. The enemy was gathering and would soon come at them in some strength; it was time, they felt, to begin the withdrawal to the beach. There was, however, a very distinct obstacle to such a move, which was beginning to become very clear to Frost: the beach and its exit were still in enemy hands. A further worry was also giving the major some concern, the No. 38 radio sets were not working and no contact had been made with the rescue boats.

Down in the valley the noise of the fighting was reaching a crescendo. Ross's men were pinned down on the 'friendly' side of the road, unable to reach the beach, and needed some support. After a few minutes of stalemate, support did finally arrive, but it did not come in the form of reinforcements from the rear but from an unlikely direction. Lieutenant Charteris and his 20 men had arrived on the other side of the road in the village. They were now mixing it with elements of the German garrison fighting their way through the rear of the houses, closing on their original objective.

In the Villa Stella Maris one of the Germans was manning the telephone line. The battalion commander rang and asked what was happening. There was much activity around the villa. Men were coming into the house and taking grenades and tracer ammunition out to the defences along the road and onto the high ground. The operator told his commander that the beach section was coming under a lot of fire from the British. The commander asked for the Feldwebel to come to the telephone to speak to him, but the telephone operator could not get out of the door to look for him for the whole building seemed to be sprayed by light machine-gun fire.

One hundred and eighty metres away Sergeant Sharp was in position near the wire keeping the enemy heads down with Sten gun fire. Above the din he heard the shout, 'Cabar Feidh!' echoing across the valley. It was the war cry of the Seaforth Highlanders and he knew that Lieutenant Charteris and his men had arrived and were launching their attack against the troublesome German defences. Sharp and his men, accompanied by Sergeant Tasker and his section, who had cleared the casemates on the northern cliff, pumped a steady stream of Sten gunfire against those Germans manning the beach defences and roadblock.

This was the turning point in the battle, for fire now came at the enemy from both sides of the road and from the centre. At last some definite progress towards capturing the escape route was beginning to materialize, but it took a while for this news to reach those up at the radar site.

Major Frost could hear the massive firefight that was taking place down at sea level and decided it was time to pull out. He gave the order for Lieutenant Vernon to get his men and the captured equipment down to the beach. The trolleys were loaded with the radar equipment and the lieutenant, Sergeant Cox and the other sappers started making their precarious way down the steep icy slopes. They had not gone far when movement came to a halt and they were told to take cover. The enemy were still in control of the beach defences ahead of them. Company Sergeant-Major Strachan was in the lead of the party when they neared the pillbox on the crest of the hill leading down to the road. As the sergeant passed the German position he was

An assault landing craft pulling alongside the *Prinz Albert* in the Solent after its return from Bruneval. The blackened faces of the Welsh commandos who gave supporting fire during the embarkation can be clearly seen. (IWM H17363)

The northern cliff overlooking the beach. On the extreme top of the picture one of the three 1942 casemates can be seen outlined against the sky. The site of the Würzburg and the villa is just over the crest of the hill. It was down these near precipitous slopes, at the time covered with ice and snow, that Sergeant Cox and the sappers had to manhandle the captured equipment to the beach. (Ken Ford)

FEBRUARY 28 1942

0235hrs The landing craft arrive at the beach

hit in the stomach by machine-gun fire coming from the high ground south of the beach road. No further movement was possible past this point through the welter of enemy fire and the withdrawal was stopped.

Major Frost came forward to deal with the situation as Strachan was given morphine and pulled behind the casemate for protection. The enemy gun opened up each time anyone moved around the crest of the cliff. It was clear that circumstances down below were far from settled. Frost was about to dispatch a runner to order Lieutenant Timothy to send a section up to the high ground opposite when things turned nasty in his rear. Word had come down to him that the Germans had occupied the villa and were advancing against him from that direction. The original enemy reinforcements from La Poterie had believed that the main aim of the landings was to attack and destroy the Freya site and had deployed to prevent this. It now became clear to them that the Würzburg was the target and that the British were pulling out. With no reserve to hand it was down to Frost to retrace his steps with the men he could muster and deal with the growing threat to his rear; these included Lieutenant Vernon and his sappers.

Lieutenant Vernon later described the scene: 'On reaching the crest of the hill we found that the beach defences were still occupied by the Germans contrary to the original plan. We were stopped half-way down the hill and told we could not go further. I then abandoned all the tools except one bag and left Sergeant Cox and the trolleys, ordering him to get them on to the ship. I then left the party and went to the top of the hill with the party of infantry to hold the crest.'

Frost led his men with what weapons they could carry, mainly Sten guns and grenades, to deal with the enemy counterattack. Fortunately the boldness shown by the enemy, which had grown when they detected the British were pulling out, soon evaporated as the paratroopers came back up the hill with all guns blazing. Many took fright and retreated whilst others sought some form of shelter and became pinned down by Frost's men. When he felt that the situation had stabilized, Frost returned down the cliff edge to the casemate and was greeted by the good news that the troublesome machine-gun opposite had been silenced. The battle down at sea level had swung in favour of the attackers, thanks to the intervention of Lieutenant Charteris and his wayward group.

Charteris and his men were pumped up for action when they came storming through the village. The enemy was scattered and did not know which way to face, nor could they work out what the paratrooper's objective was. The British were everywhere, firing like mad and silencing anyone who showed themselves. Charteris led his men across the road, down the valley and through the barbed-wire barricades barring the beach exit. One section peeled off to the right and swept up to the Germans holding the south cliff, while the others made their way towards the beach, now joined by Captain Ross and his men. The sappers immediately got to work sweeping the shore and the route down to it with mine detectors; they found none. Opposition on the hill was soon eliminated, including the machine-gun that had hit Sergeant Strachan.

In the villa on the beach the German telephone operator stuck by his instrument, which seemed to be ringing every few minutes. On the line was an irate major 'in the last stages of agitation', recalled the operator. 'The major told me not to make so much noise. I explained that the noise was caused by grenades coming through the window and bursting all around me, whereupon he told me to withdraw.' The unfortunate German could not, however, safely get out of the building for the British were all around him. He turned out the light and went into an inner room and hid. A few moments later paratroopers burst in, firing their Stens. The room was in darkness and the German could see the British but they could not see him. 'I wondered whether I should fire, but could not bring myself to shoot into a man's body at a range of a few yards. I therefore surrendered.'

Up on the north cliff Sergeant Cox could now resume his task of getting his captured booty down to the beach. It was hard going, for the trolleys slipped and slid at all angles over the icy slopes, causing the sappers to curse and struggle with the cumbersome transport. Cox and his men had a solution: 'We found that the equipment could be carried much better on our shoulders than by trolley, so the trolleys were abandoned. We made our way down to the beach and found we had to wait, so we stowed the equipment in a safe position under the cliff and, as there was nothing else we could do, we just sat down and waited.'

FEBRUARY 28
1942

**0315hrs
The last landing
craft withdraws
from the
beach**

FEBRUARY 28
1942

**0335hrs
Landing craft
rendezvous with
MGBs**

FEBRUARY 28
1942

**0800hrs
Spitfire fighters
provide air cover
for flotilla**

Flight Sergeant Cox alongside an army corporal, possibly the sapper Corporal Jones, describes his part in the raid to Sir Nigel Norman, the Air Commander of Operation *Biting*. Cox's expertise as a radar technician proved to be vitally important during the dismantling of the German radar. (Crown Copyright)

The Withdrawal

The beach was captured, the paratroopers were arriving on the shore, but there was no sign of the navy. Major Frost later recorded what he felt at that moment: 'There was now time to take stock. So far the object had been achieved. We had very few casualties. We knew roughly where everybody was. We had given the enemy a good hammering and so far they had produced no effective counter-measures. It was about quarter-past two in the morning. All we wanted now was the navy.'

The navy were out there, waiting just offshore, but they were puzzled by the silence from the raiders and were not sure whether or not the beach was safe to come in to. Frost's men had with them both No. 18 and No. 38 radios, none of which seemed to be working. The No. 18 set was specifically provided for contacting the landing craft and it had been planned that once the beach had been captured contact was to be made with Commander Cook's craft for embarkation to begin. Both Charteris and Ross carried the radios in their sections. Their signallers had been trying for almost two hours to make contact, as had the sappers with their Rebecca portable radio beacon, all with no success. Time was slipping by and the tide was falling, bringing back fears of the last exercise in Southampton Water before the raid, when the boats became grounded on an ebb tide whilst taking off the paratroopers.

Word had gone out from Frost to all units for them to begin the general withdrawal to the beach. All those men holding rearguard positions were to steadily fall back to be ready for embarkation. Lieutenant Timothy's group reported that headlights had been seen approaching Bruneval from the east and south-east, indicating that heavy German reinforcements were moving against the landings. With no sign of the landing craft, the major reluctantly gave the order to establish a defensive perimeter to meet the inevitable German attack on the beach. He was asking his men to defend a position against the inevitable. The moment the enemy brought heavier weapons into play, especially mortars, the operation would be over; surrender would be the only option.

The beach was now becoming full of men pulling back from contact with the enemy. It was still reasonably safe, for those few remaining enemy troops from the Bruneval and Le Presbytère garrisons had been given such treatment by the raiders that they remained cautious of pressing the British too closely. Captain Ross suggested to Major Frost that perhaps they could signal to the boats with Very lights. The major thought it was worth a try and allowed a green light to be sent up from the north of the beach simultaneously with another, this time a red one, from the south. As first there was no reaction, so another volley of flares was fired. This time there was a response, for the move turned out to be just what the navy wanted, reasoning that the signals surely meant that the beach was safe and two landing craft started to run into shore. When they were about 275m out the incoming craft picked up a strong signal from one of the raider's No. 38 sets. Without waiting for authority, the jubilant signaller operating the set called for all the craft to come in. Word quickly went round to the men waiting on the beach and up to those crouched along the defensive perimeter: 'The navy's here!' It was 0235hrs and C Company had been fighting for over two hours.

As the landing craft rode the surf into the beach the Welsh commandos onboard each of the vessels opened fire on the area inland and the cliffs

OVERLEAF
Men from Captain Ross' and Lieutenant Charteris' groups attack the enemy pillbox and roadblock that guarded the approach to Bruneval beach. German resistance to the landings was stiffer than expected and had delayed this assault on the last few metres of the withdrawal route. The late arrival of Charteris and his men in the village had also put embarkation behind schedule. For a short time the possibility of a successful outcome to the whole enterprise looked in doubt. At that moment enemy reinforcements were approaching the village from the north-east and the garrison at Le Presbytère was pressing the northern perimeter of the lodgement. As each minute passed, the likelihood grew of more troops and heavier weapons being brought against the raiders. It was fortunate that the momentum of one final brave assault on the enemy position carried Frost's men through the obstructions and on to the beach, freeing up a route to the landing craft and eventual safety.

flanking the shore with their Bren guns. This was quickly stopped by a frantic radio message, for many of Frost's men were still holding the ground and were in the way of this light machine-gun fire. Frost had planned for the landing craft to come in two at a time and for the embarkation to take place in an orderly manner. This did not happen. The arrival of all six craft in the surf was the signal for the perimeter to contract and for everyone to head for the boats.

First, and most importantly, Cox and the sappers came forward with the German radar equipment. Every man on the beach knew that the sappers had to get the captured booty away and this particular embarkation took priority along with the evacuation of the wounded. The paras had also learned a thing or two from the many boat practices during training and now put their seamanship into practice. Men were quickly in the surf to hold the landing craft stern-on to the sea whilst the remainder helped each other to board the swirling pitching craft. The swell and the falling tide made the manoeuvre quite a challenge, but the adrenalin of battle still pumped through their veins and the end of the operation was now close. Soon they would be away from the prospect of sudden death.

Enemy reinforcements were now gathering in Bruneval and the sound of the naval craft down on the beach signalled to them that the British were pulling out. As the embarkation process dragged on and more and more of the raiders came back to the beach Germans began sniping at them from the two cliffs on either side. For the most part they were held at bay by the Bren guns of the Welsh commandos posted on the landing craft. When each of the ALCs was full it backed away. Their numbers gradually fell as each craft got their complement on board until just the last one remained. A call was shouted for any last men and, when no reply came, the final landing craft pulled back at 0315hrs and headed out to sea, sent on its way by volleys of enemy fire from the shore.

The first of the ALCs away from Bruneval took the wounded, together with Cox and the sappers. Once clear of the inland waters and well into the comforting cover of darkness, the craft met up with the waiting Fairmile C Class Motor Gun Boat MGB 312. Whilst the two light vessels bobbed around on an increasingly rough sea, the radar equipment and the landing craft's passengers were transferred to the powerful motor boat. Once all was safely stowed on board, the master of MGB 312 opened up its three 850hp (630kW) supercharged Hall-Scott petrol engines and made off for Portsmouth at more than 20 knots

The remaining five landing craft also rendezvoused with Commander Cook's MGBs and transferred their now wet passengers to the larger craft. By 0335hrs the powerful inshore motor boats were under way, towing the more ungainly landing craft for home at a maximum speed of just seven knots. Progress was slow and by the first light of dawn the convoy was still only 24km off the coast of France. It was very uncomfortable below decks for the rescued parachutists, most especially as the wind had risen to Force 5 and the boats were pitching and rolling badly, but they were at least dry and warm and tucking into some good food. At around 0800hrs the familiar drone of Merlin engines was heard from above, and a protective screen of Spitfire fighters from No. 11 Group swept low in greeting, then banked round and round to shepherd the small craft home. Soon a rendezvous was made with four Free French *chasseurs*, the *Bayonne*, *Calais*, *Larmor* and the *Le Lavandou*, circling the craft providing extra protection. Not to be outdone on such a momentous occasion, the Royal Navy also turned up with the destroyers HMS *Blencathra* and HMS *Fernie*, offering to escort the conquering heroes back to base.

On board MGB 312 was Donald Priest, the scientist from the Telecommunications Research Establishment at Swanage. As soon as the captured radio equipment was aboard he began examining the electronic components and questioning Vernon and Cox. The flight sergeant remarked to the scientist that he thought the whole installation was beautifully made and finely engineered, indicating to Priest that the enemy must be far ahead of them in radar production. Priest was inclined to agree with him but told the airman to keep such thoughts 'under his hat'.

Also on board the motor boat were the wounded who had been rescued from the battle: eight men, including Company Sergeant-Major Strachan. Seven other men were unaccounted for and had been left in France. One of them, Private Scott, was originally listed among those missing, but it was later discovered that he had been killed during the fighting. Two of those who did not make it back to the boats were signallers and Frost was later distressed to hear that they were signalling to the landing craft as the boats pulled out to sea.

At 0815hrs Commander Cook was able to signal to the Commander-in-Chief Portsmouth that the raid had been a triumph and all craft were present and returning to port. News quickly spread around the dockyard of the spectacular nature of the operation and its complete success. The press and many important people now made themselves ready to welcome home the victors. First to arrive off Spithead was MGB 312, with the RDF equipment and technical experts on board. After its high-speed passage from France it pulled alongside the *Prinz Albert* at around 1000hrs. The remainder of Commander Cook's flotilla returned at a leisurely seven knots, towing the ungainly landing craft, and arrived in the Solent at 1630hrs. Just before they entered the sheltered waters the French *chasseurs*, followed by the two British destroyers, swept by and saluted the slow-moving craft. Then the Spitfires swooped low overhead with their own gesture of recognition to the raiders. By 1800hrs the survivors of the raid were all safely aboard the mother ship being fêted as heroes and basking in the realization of a job well done.

As with all clashes with the enemy, there was a price to pay. Privates McIntyre and Scott had been killed and their bodies left in France; eight other men had returned as casualties. Six of the raiders were missing, presumed captured. Major-General Browning's report written shortly after the operation claimed that a minimum of 40 enemy had been killed. Enemy reports captured after the war show this to be an exaggeration, for the German Army claimed it lost two killed, one seriously wounded and two

The MGB carrying Major Frost arrives back in home waters. The familiar moustached face of Frost can be seen on the bridge in front of the craft's mast. (Crown Copyright)

FEBRUARY 28 1942

0815hrs Commander Cook signals the mission's success

missing – the two brought back to England – and that there were three Luftwaffe killed, one wounded and three missing, only one of whom was brought back with the raiders. Perhaps the other two had taken the opportunity to escape from the service.

ANALYSIS

Major Frost and the men of C Company returned to Tilshead Camp late on Saturday night ready for some well-earned leave. So great had been the security before the raid that the glider pilots resident at the camp had no idea that the men who carried out the raid, news of which was in all the papers, had been living with them for the past six weeks. The next day they rested, cleaned themselves and their equipment, and once more assumed the smart demeanour of soldiers. A detailed debriefing was to be held later so that lessons could be learned and tactics evaluated, but for the moment the men just enjoyed the temporary peace allowed after standing down from a mission. A *post mortem* had to be held, for it was important in this first successful British parachute operation of the war to understand what went right and what went wrong. However before Frost could put all this into place, he was summoned to London for a very important meeting.

At 2100hrs on Monday 2 March, Major-General Browning, accompanied by his General Staff Officer (GSO) 1 and Major Frost, was called to give an account of Operation *Biting* to the War Cabinet. The meeting was held in the underground Cabinet War Rooms, located at the back of the Treasury Building in Birdcage Walk. An impressive array of top brass and political leaders were present to hear the briefing. Prominent in the room was the Prime Minister Winston Churchill, dressed quite casually in a siren suit and smoking a cigar. Also there were the three Chiefs of Staff: the Chief of the Imperial General Staff, General Sir Alan Brooke; the First Sea Lord, Admiral of the Fleet Sir Dudley Pound and the Chief of the Air Staff, Air Chief Marshal Sir Charles Portal. In addition the Deputy Prime Minister, Clement Atlee, the Foreign Secretary, Anthony Eden and the Commander Combined Operations, Lord Louis Mountbatten, were also in attendance, as were the various Secretaries of State for the three services.

Major-General Browning and Lord Mountbatten outlined the raid and the circumstances leading up to it. When he was finished he introduced Major Frost. 'Bravo Frost,' exclaimed the Prime Minister. 'Now we must hear all about it.' The major told of his part in the operation – much more exciting to Churchill than the bare facts given by Browning – and then Churchill asked

FEBRUARY 28
1942

1630hrs
The flotilla
arrives in the
Solent

his Chief of Air Staff what it was he hoped to get out of the raid. Portal began a technical explanation of how the captured equipment would help in the battle for radar supremacy, but the scientific details soon left Churchill floundering and the Prime Minster asked Portal to keep it simple. Churchill seemed to enjoy the briefing and he urged his Chiefs of Staff, and Mountbatten in particular, to plan and execute more raids like Operation *Biting*. He left the room in a high state of elation, content that his forces had breached the walls of Hitler's Fortress Europe with impunity. This excitement also was shared by the nation when details of the raid were released to the newspapers.

Earlier that day, Dr R. V. Jones paid a visit to the Air Ministry to see the captured German equipment taken in the raid. As with all the scientists that examined the apparatus, he was immediately struck with the quality of the engineering work that went into its construction; it was well ahead of British equipment. Once he had studied what had been brought back he was quick to acknowledge that the raiders had done a very good job. Flight Sergeant Cox, Lieutenant Vernon and Corporal Jones had recovered some remarkable pieces and the only thing missing was the presentation and display equipment, but Frost's men had brought back the next best thing, a German radar operator who could describe its details.

The prisoner proved to be very talkative and quite content to answer any questions put to him. Of course, there was a very real possibility that the captive would try to lead his interrogators astray, but this particular German individual seemed to be unable to act in a disingenuous manner and was willing to impart all that he knew. The prisoner was one of life's losers and seemed to have spent more of his adult life on the inside of prisons than on the outside. The man was a reserve operator and commented that his colleagues knew much more than he did and would have been of more help, but the raiders had shot them. It soon became clear that the German was of limited intelligence. He was unable during his training to master Morse code and even after two months of practical experience on the Würzburg he still believed that the instrument 'saw' the aircraft in some way and was consequently less effective in bad weather. His technical competence was far lower that comparable British operators. Despite the naivety of the prisoner Jones and the scientist were able to extract a great deal of useful information about the operation of the radar system, the processes associated with its maintenance and the layout of the Würzburg and Freya sites. A later report on the interrogation came to the following conclusion: 'The prisoner was rather childlike and extremely unsoldierly in mentality. It is probable that with time he would have acquired considerable manual skill in following a target with his apparatus, but it is quite certain that he would never have understood its working; the slightest abnormal event would either cause him to declare his apparatus unserviceable, or (more probably) to continue cheerfully taking totally erroneous observations.'

The low skill level obtained by the prisoner and the high standard of manufacture of the equipment were an indication of how Germany approached its radar systems. It would appear that a low priority was given to demands for personnel and the service had to make do with those not suitable for other more challenging duties. Unlike the British, the Nazis could not call upon a vast network of radio amateurs amongst its population, for Hitler had banned amateur radio after coming to power. The dictator did not like the idea of his people having unfettered communication with those of other countries. Therefore with a low skill base using and maintaining the radar equipment, the apparatus had to be relatively simple to operate and easy to replace any part that broke down. Its modular assembly assisted this process, for if one section of the equipment failed to work correctly, it was simply removed and replaced by a spare.

Much information was also gained by looking at the serial numbers on the equipment. As each part had been replaced through failure or by being updated, its works number and the date it was changed was added to it. From a study of these numbers the scientists concluded that the manufacturer Telefunken was producing around 150 sets per month. If a third of these were designated as spares, it meant that the Germans were producing around 100 new Würzburgs for installation per month.

The information also implied that the Bruneval installation was an early type, at least two years old, which would indicate that the enemy had by 1942 developed a much more sophisticated set in the intervening years. The scientists at TRE then compared the apparatus with equipment contemporary to 1939/1940, rather than their own latest equipment.

They concluded that the Würzburg circuit design and performance were straightforward rather than ingenious or brilliant and nothing was found that was novel. Their report summed up the differences: 'We did not achieve a range of 40 Km on a 50 Cm wavelength against aircraft until 1941, nor did we incorporate common transmitter/receiver equipment in 1939 designs. The nearest equivalent in our own performances would be that of GL Mk II, but the enemy has achieved this performance with far simpler equipment. While the circuit design is simple, the engineering design and construction are outstanding. We may study this to our advantage.'

Now that the scientists at TRE had a comprehensive knowledge of the Würzburg, serious thought could be given to finding means to jam the device or to neutralize its performance. An understanding of its operation led to the use of 'window' later in the war, a process whereby thousands of small aluminium strips were dropped to reflect radar waves and make it appear that a great number of aircraft were in the sky. Details of the operational intercommunication between the Freya and Würzburg sites also suggested that if intruders came in low across the Channel they might get under the Freya beams and cross the coast unseen, for although the Würzburg would be able to spot these aircraft, they would not have been alerted by the Freya station to look for them. From a technical viewpoint, the raid was a complete and invaluable exercise.

The military assessment of Operation *Biting* came to the same conclusion. The air, land and sea operations were all successful. Combined Operations HQ had put together a plan that had worked almost to perfection. All three services had co-ordinated well although, at times, things did not go altogether as planned, but none of the unforeseen events that cropped up had compromised the mission to any appreciable degree. In the main the aircraft had dropped the parachutists on time on target – the two sticks that dropped prematurely were close enough to the drop zone to rejoin the main force and take part in the operation. There were problems contacting the landing craft, but these were eventually solved by a combination of persistence and determination. The embarkation was not as orderly as planned, but all the men on the beach got away.

The successful outcome of this first parachute operation across the Channel proved that there was a future for airborne forces both as raiders and invaders. Over the next two years the Parachute Regiment expanded and a second airborne division was raised. Better air transport was developed and special units trained to fly them. No longer could RAF Bomber Command be asked to provide ancient bombers for the task. By the time of the Normandy invasion, Britain had the men and the equipment to carry out large-scale airborne operations against the enemy.

These positive actions in England after the raid were mirrored across the Channel by the enemy, although many of his moves were actually to British advantage. An intelligence report written in the months following Operation *Biting* clearly shows how the enemy played into British hands: 'The Bruneval raid evidently activated the local defence officer, for within a few weeks the field around the site had been effectively covered with an entangled pattern of barbed wire exceeding in complexity anything yet seen on any other military site.' The Würzburg was removed and re-erected within the Freya compound. A further result of the raid was that every German radio station near the coast became conscious of its vulnerability and surrounded itself with masses of barbed wire. 'This actually helped us,' went on the report, 'for there were several sites which were formerly suspected to contain Würzburgs which were insufficiently distinct on existing photographs to be identified. The Germans have now obligingly surrounded these sites with wire and have

Paratroopers disembark from an MGB after arriving back in home waters after the mission. (IWM 17359)

confirmed our suspicions.' As the war progressed many military sites were located from the air by conspicuous areas of long grass that remained within the barbed-wire perimeters, for grazing cattle loose outside the compound could not get at the grass to keep it neatly trimmed. The report also added, 'This method of betrayal might well be noticed by those responsible for camouflaging our own stations.'

One of the minor objectives of the raid was to destroy the villa at Bruneval located alongside the radar. The building was thought to be a headquarters and its destruction by the raiders was planned to interfere with the work of the site. In the event this did not happen during the raid for lack of time. The Germans however, must have thought its presence too prominent a landmark, for six weeks after the operation they demolished it.

The ease at which Bruneval was raided led to some serious thinking with relation to British radar establishments, for it was reasonably agreed that Operation *Biting* might sting the Germans into retaliation. The enemy certainly showed increasing interest in the Telecommunications Research Establishment at Swanage, which suffered several minor air raids and was probably photographed extensively. British air photographs of the TRE site clearly showed it to be an air reconnaissance interpreter's paradise. The parabolic reflectors on the site showed up from 9,150m, as did the many other installations around Swanage. This caused a great scare within the scientific hierarchy. When it was reported that a German paratroop company had moved to Cherbourg just across the Channel from Dorset, the action prompted a decision to be made to remove the TRE establishment to a safe place well inland. Three months after the Bruneval raid a start was made on moving TRE from Swanage to Malvern in Worcestershire.

CONCLUSION

There was no doubt in the minds of everyone involved in Operation *Biting* that the raid had been a complete success. The day after the homecoming the newspapers were full of details about the audacious enterprise against enemy-occupied territory. The main object of the operation was kept from the public, for there had still been no general disclosure that the country possessed radar and it remained a closely guarded secret for the rest of the war. Nonetheless, people could at last celebrate what was a carefully planned and executed force of arms and a demonstration of the country's ability to strike back at Hitler's forces. It was the first armed landing in German-occupied Europe and it showed that Britain had fully trained airborne forces equal to those of the enemy. 'Bruneval' became the first battle honour of the newly formed Parachute Regiment.

A German report on the raid acknowledged its success as a military venture: 'The operation of the British commandos was well planned and was executed with great daring. During the operation the British displayed exemplary discipline when under fire. Although attacked by German soldiers they concentrated entirely on their primary task. For a full thirty minutes one group did not fire a shot, then suddenly at the sound of a whistle they went into action.'

The Bruneval Raid has quite naturally been seen as a great triumph for the Parachute Regiment. Combined Operations HQ should also be given the same accolade, for Operation *Biting* was the result of much meticulous organization by its planners. Bruneval was just one of the great raids prepared by Mountbatten's team that year: Operation *Biting* was followed by Operation *Chariot*, the commando raid on the dry docks at Saint-Nazaire in March and Operation *Jubilee*, the major landings at Dieppe in August.

The site today has changed dramatically since 1942 and is probably one of the least interesting battlefields that the author has visited. After the villa was demolished the area was fortified with a number of bunkers and defence positions. These great monoliths were all blown up after the war and remain just a jumble of reinforced concrete shells. A few post-raid Tobruk positions are scattered across the landscape and the rectangle of woods around the

This monument to those who took part in Operation *Biting* is situated on the site of the German defences located on the high ground to the south of the beach. (Ken Ford)

buildings of Le Presbytère now house crumbling German gun emplacements. The ground over which Major Frost led his paratroopers that snowy February night has been given over to grazing cattle, corralled into certain grassy patches by a criss-cross maze of electric cow fences. '*Interdit*' notices everywhere warn the visitor that it is prohibited to stray onto the land, though there is no real point in doing so for nothing remains from the time of the raid.

Down at the beach a straightened road, an ugly reinforced sea wall, a modern house and areas of bland concrete make it impossible to try to recreate in one's mind's eye the events of more than half a century ago. On the south cliff is a recent monument to the raid. On the top of the north cliff the outline of one of the German casemates can be seen perched high up on the path that leads down to sea level, although only the very brave would attempt to reach it along so precipitous and dangerous a route.

SOURCES AND FURTHER READING

There has only ever been one full book on Operation *Biting*, George Millar's *The Bruneval Raid* (The Bodley Head, London), published in 1974. Hilary St George Saunders produced a book on the Parachute Regiment in 1950 called *The Red Beret* (Michael Joseph, London), which included a chapter on the Bruneval Raid. The book is excellent for information on the origins of the Parachute Regiment, but the section on Operation *Biting* has many errors and omissions. In 1978 R.V. Jones released his autobiography, *Most Secret War* (Hamish Hamilton, London), containing much information on the beginnings of British radar and his part in the location of the Würzburg at Bruneval.

For those interested in the early development of radar two books are of note: *Winning the Radar War* (Robert Hale, London, 1989), written by Jack Nissen with A.W. Cockerill and *Instruments of Darkness* (William Kimber, London, 1967) by Alfred Price.

Many original reports and documents relating to the Bruneval Raid and the captured German radar equipment can be found in the National Archives at Kew in London. The principal documents used in the preparation of this book are listed below.

AIR 8/867	Operation *Biting*
AIR 32/8	Training for combined operations: Operation *Biting*
AIR 39/43	Operation *Biting*
AIR 40/3057	Intelligence aspects of Operation *Biting*
AVIA 26/1872	German RDF equipment captured at Bruneval, 28 Feb 1942
DEFE 40/2	Operational research reports; reports on enemy radio activity; intelligence aspects of the Bruneval Raid (capture of the Würzburg apparatus)
PREMIER 3/73	*Biting* operation (Bruneval raid)
WO 106/4133	Report by Major-General Browning on Operation *Biting*

INDEX